Think in patterns of the Tao,
And your spirit will travel far.

—Liu Hsieh

A Taoist hat, Confucian shoes,
and a Buddhist robe combine
the Three Houses into one.

—*Zenrin kushu*

Dedicated to
Ichikawa Takashi:
Friend, mentor, recluse, mountaineer.

Distributed in the United States by Kodansha America, LLC, and in the United Kingdom and continental Europe by Kodansha Europe Ltd.

Published by Kodansha International Ltd., 17–14 Otowa 1-chome, Bunkyo-ku, Tokyo 112–8652.

ISBN 978–4–7700–3097–9

First edition, 2009
18 17 16 15 14 13 12 11 10 09   10 9 8 7 6 5 4 3 2 1

Library of Congress Cataloging-in-Publication Data

Hong, Zicheng, fl. 1596
[Cai gen tan. English]
The unencumbered spirit : reflections of a Chinese sage / by Hung Ying-ming ; translated by William Scott Wilson ; with a foreword by Bill Porter (Red Pine). -- 1st ed.
p. cm.
Revised translation of: The Roots of wisdom : Saikontan. 1985.
Includes bibliographical references.
ISBN 978-4-7700-3097-9 (alk. paper)
1. Conduct of life. I. Wilson, William Scott, 1944- Roots of wisdom. II. Title.

BJ1588.C5H8613 2009
181'.11--dc22

2009025154

www.kodansha-intl.com

CONTENTS

FOREWORD

When I open a book as ancient and profound as *The Unencumbered Spirit*, I can't help but be carried back to where the traditions so perfectly represented on its pages began. Invariably, I find myself traveling toward the Yellow River.

A million or so years ago, the Yellow River began dumping mud into the ocean one summer storm at a time. With the uplifting of the Tibetan Plateau and the disappearance of annual monsoons, North China became increasingly arid. Lush forests became grasslands, grasslands became deserts, and every summer the deserts washed into the river that debouched an empire of mud into the ocean, an empire that eventually stretched from Beijing in the north to Loyang in the south and from the Taihang Mountains in the west to the Pohai Sea in the east. In the absence of mountain terrain and primeval forests, nomadic hunter-gatherers couldn't have found an easier place to make the transition to farming and permanent settlements. It was along the edges of this vast floodplain of 150,000 square miles of alluvial mud that Chinese civilization first arose 5,000 years ago. It is no coincidence that is also where we find the birthplaces and graves of the men and women to whom the Chinese still look as their greatest sages.

Eighty miles south of where the Yellow River bends northeast across this vast floodplain and makes its final push to the sea was where China's first sages held court around 3300 B.C. At a place called

Huaiyang, Fu Hsi and his wife Nu Wa established the capital that marked the beginning of Chinese history—even if it was of the semi-legendary variety. It was Nu Wa (Noah) who saved everyone from the Great Flood. And it was her husband Fu Hsi who devised the trigrams that formed the basis of the *I Ching*, or *Book of Changes*. Several centuries later, Huaiyang also became the seat of power of Shen Nung, who is honored as the father of Chinese agriculture and also Chinese medicine. As Chinese legend became Chinese history, one sage followed another in and around Huaiyang. Among them was Lao Tzu, patriarch of Taoism and author of the *Tao Te Ching*, who was born forty miles east of Huaiyang, and Chuang Tzu, the second-most important figure in Taoism and author of the book that bears his name, whose hometown was only sixty miles north of Lao Tzu's.

Given their temporal proximity to their Neolithic forebears, it shouldn't be surprising that these early sages were astute observers of the natural world and its interaction with the human body. But unlike in other parts of the world, where the heavy hand of monotheism marginalized, if not demonized, the cultivation of such awareness, in the Yellow River floodplain this became the polestar that guided the new rulers of China's Middle Kingdom.

Over time, such study and practice resulted in what the Chinese still call their only native religious tradition, namely that of Taoism. But as Taoism arose out of this sea of Yellow River mud, so did another tradition, one that was less religious but no less important in guiding people's lives. One hundred and fifty miles northeast of where Lao Tzu was born was the home of Confucius.

In the shadow of Taishan, China's most sacred mountain and the place where departed spirits go for assignment to their next existence, Confucius reflected on the workings not of the natural world and the human body but of society and human relationships, and produced the ethical system known as Confucianism. Over the centuries that followed, Confucianism joined Taoism in the firmament to which all Chinese, both rulers and subjects, looked for guidance.

But something was missing. Conducting their lives on the basis of a knowledge of the body and society did not lead to the peace and happiness people hoped for. It wasn't until the beginning of the Christian era that the missing ingredient arrived. That missing ingredient was Buddhism, with its focus not on the body and the natural world, nor on the workings of society and human relationships. Its focus, instead, was on the mind and the suffering that arises from its misuse. Over the course of the following centuries, these three traditions dominated China's religious, spiritual, ethical, intellectual, and even its literary landscape. And together they became the source of the Path that all Chinese followed.

As Chinese civilization spread south from the Yellow River into the Yangtze watershed of Central China and later into the West River watershed of South China, it brought with it these three traditions as an inextricable part of its own fabric. To be Chinese was to cultivate the Way of Lao Tzu, the Way of Confucius, and the Way of the Buddha. Unlike other such traditions in the world that demanded the extermination of rival schools of belief and practice, the Chinese saw these not as conflicting traditions, but as complementary. Hence, the teachings of Lao Tzu, Confucius, and the Buddha have remained the mainstay of Chinese culture ever since, the teachings of Marx and Mao and lately Adam Smith notwithstanding.

Even where individuals have chosen to emphasize one over the others in their own lives, they have rarely turned their back on the others. This is because they have recognized that each addresses a different aspect of the human condition: Taoism seeks the harmony of the body, Confucianism seeks the harmony of society, and Buddhism seeks the harmony of the mind.

But even though it can be said that the Chinese people have

honored and cultivated all three traditions, and even though they have incorporated various aspects of each into their lives, it has been rare for one person to develop a thorough grasp of all three, such is their individual profundity. But there have been a few. Among them, one person's work stands above the rest: namely, Hung Ying-ming's *The Unencumbered Spirit*. It was with great delight that I recently learned that my old friend Bill Wilson had undertaken a new translation of this classic of Chinese thought. And it is with great pleasure that I now recommend this work to anyone interested in the way of the world's greatest sages, whose teachings can help us all to see into and to improve our own lives. Someone once asked Confucius to define the Tao. He said, "The Tao is what you can never leave. What you can leave isn't the Tao." So here we are. Back home again.

Bill Porter / Red Pine
Port Townsend, Washington

INTRODUCTION

The Unencumbered Spirit is perhaps the very finest literary expression of the Unity of the Three Creeds—Confucianism, Ch'an (Zen) Buddhism, and Taoism. Composed of three hundred and fifty-seven verses of accessible prose-poetry, it not only expresses the root values of the three traditions while rarely mentioning them by name, but also takes as points of departure the branches of these philosophies as expressed by other Chinese poets and philosophers. As such, it is a *tour de force* of Chinese tradition expressed in a very palatable form, a product of over two millennia of rumination on, and digestion of, three of the most profound thought-systems in human history. And, in Chinese history, it appeared at a fortuitous time.

At the end of the sixteenth century, the Chinese were faced with a number of daunting problems: an incompetent, feckless, and detached leadership; a corrupt administration; factional strife within the government itself; a squandering of the national treasury; and fiscal bankruptcy. Added to this list of woes were military actions against foreign countries, problems with the incursion of foreigners at national borders, and what was perceived by some as the degradation of traditional values.

Various responses to the civil unrest and disorder ensued. A conservative group of Confucian scholars, the Tung-lin Academy, conducted a crusade to reinstate what they felt were the core moral values of traditional Chinese society. They denounced the Unity of the Three Creeds movement, prevalent at that time, which saw Taoism, Confucianism, and Buddhism as a single philosophy; they condemned officials whom they felt to be lacking in moral integrity and virtue. At the same time, there were officials who attempted to reform the tax structure and the privileges of the upper classes. At the extreme, there were outright rebellions. All the movements—conservative or otherwise—responding to the governmental and economic failures were based on a reaction to the times, a call to change. Not to act, it was supposed, meant to fall behind.

There were a few people during this tumultuous period, however, who chose not to become involved. Such men reasoned that, rather than living in reaction to the changing times, it would be preferable to transcend them. They argued that, rather than jockeying in competition with others for power and influence, living in relative obscurity would be infinitely more satisfying and would put one in contact with his or her true being. And rather than grasping for monetary and material gain, a life of simplicity and plain living would make one far more content with life and would engender a healthier lifestyle as well.

One such man was Hung Ying-ming, a recluse or near recluse living in the mountains of southeastern China near the lower Yangtze River, and the author of *The Unencumbered Spirit* (Chinese: *Ts'ai Ken T'an*; Japanese: *Saikontan*). Almost nothing is known of Hung. A reading of his book, however, reveals that he was remarkably well educated; that he used his education not to get ahead in business or government, but to sharpen his perceptions and give depth to his understanding of the world; and that he was deeply versed in Confucianism, Taoism, and Zen Buddhism.

It is also clear that he was one of the literati, or *wen-jen* (Japanese: *bunjin*), a class of men—and likely women—who preferred to spend their time reading and writing poetry, painting, practicing the martial arts, rambling through nature, and laughing and drinking with friends. Such people have often been considered simply dilettantes or escapists, or at best, artists and poets with more interest in their own creative activities than in the "real" world. This is, perhaps, an incorrect conclusion.

To understand why this is so, we must, as with many of the Oriental arts, take a step back in order to go forward.

The Source

According to ancient Chinese tradition, sometime around the year 3322 B.C., the sovereign Fu Hsi gazed upward to observe the images in Heaven, and downward to discern the images on Earth. Sometimes depicted as a leaf-wreathed head emerging from a mountain, and sometimes as a being with the head and upper torso of a man and the body of gigantean serpent, he was well suited to see through phenomena both celestial and earthbound. Fu Hsi, however, looked not only at the individual transient beings of the world, but also at the *patterns* of the birds and beasts, of the wind through the trees, and of the flowing waters. Thus, he observed the patterns of eternal change, and the continuous transformation of one pattern into another. With this understanding, he created eight trigrams, the foundation of the sixty-four hexagrams of the *I Ching*, which in turn would classify all possible conditions in the world according to their innate nature and natural course. It is through these hexagrams, through these patterns, that we may come to an understanding of the Tao.

We are interested in these universal patterns, not only because they are the ultimate expressions of *ch'i*, the material-energy or fundamental breath of the universe, but also because they are considered to be the substratum of all culture and literature in China.

Indeed, the Chinese character *wen* 文, which originally indicated intersecting strokes or criss-cross patterns on cowrie shells, straw mats, or tiger skins, later came to mean the patterns of human culture, or culture itself. Finally, it was understood as literature, which to the Chinese is culture's highest expression. All of these meanings, whether configurations of natural phenomena, the natural cultural patterns of mankind, or the literary expressions of man's mind, were and are thought to be manifestations of the Tao. In the early sixth century A.D., Liu Hsieh wrote,

> The power of *wen* . . . was born together with Heaven and Earth . . . Heaven and Earth, the sun and moon, the mountains and rivers . . . spread their orderly arrangements over the Earth—these are really the *wen* of the Tao . . . Man is the finest essence of the Five Agents [water, earth, metal, fire, and air], and truly the mind of Heaven and Earth. When mind was born, then language was established; when language was established, then *wen* [literature/patterns] shone forth. This is a natural principle [Tao].[1]

Literature, then, can be a natural manifestation of the Tao and, through the use of appropriate outward patterns, may express the universal patterns with which we must be in tune. In this way, Chung-ni's statement, "If words do not have patterns, they will not go far," should be applied to the way we live our lives as well as to how we speak or write.

The Book

The Unencumbered Spirit is a book about living with simplicity and awareness. It is a book about getting at the true taste of things without all the distracting and encumbering sauces and spices. It is a book about living without *stuff*, whether it be material, psychological, or spiritual. We start on this book with the title, because the title holds the key.

The literal meaning of the Chinese title of *The Unencumbered Spirit* is "Vegetable Root Discourses." This is thought to have been inspired by a quote from the Sung-Dynasty philosopher Wang Hsin-min that was included in the writings of Chu Hsi, the great Confucian scholar of the same dynasty:

> If one is able to chew the vegetable roots well,
> He should be able to do all things.

Chu Hsi's accompanying remark was, "In looking at the men of today, there are many who run counter even to their own true minds because they are unable to chew the vegetable roots." These quotes are to be taken on two levels. First, if we do not chew things well—that is, if we do not ruminate and contemplate things over a period of time—we will not know their true taste or have a deep understanding of them. Approaching the world without "chewing well" is what the Confucians called knowledge that "enters the ears and goes right out through the mouth." Second, the image of the vegetable root is one of radical simplicity. If we truly wish to live, it is the simplest and most fundamental things in life that will give us its true savor; that is, the true taste of life.

The Unencumbered Spirit develops this theme throughout its three hundred and fifty-seven verses, steeped in motifs from the Three Creeds and from the poets and historians of China's history. The work is divided into two books, the first one generally dealing with the art of living in society, the second concerned more with man's solitude and contemplation of nature. These themes, however, repeatedly spill over into each other, creating multiple levels of meaning in much the same way as the book's Chinese title.

Hung's writing style may be seen in the same light. He writes in what is called parallel prose (*p'ien wen* 駢文), which is in keeping with the above-mentioned Chinese sense of patterns 文, both natural and literary. This style is fashioned by using a certain number of characters in each line, thus creating parallel patterns and making the medium itself almost as much a message as the content. The images of the verses also run parallel in comparative and contrasting ideas, but Hung constantly modifies this style, much as nature modifies its own patterns, so that the reader never feels the weight of monotony or repetition.

Hung's themes are reflected in his choice of words, and a few key words require brief explanations. Some of these terms belong to the vocabulary of the Chinese classics, and I have usually translated them in accordance with earlier translations of these classics to avoid confusion, and also because they are often the best English words available for concepts that lack exact counterparts in Western culture.

Chuntzu (君子) The Gentleman: Originally meaning "prince," the term was transformed by the early Chinese philosophers to mean the ideal man, who knew both the literary and the military arts and those arts necessary for living in society. In the present work, he is a man of virtue and of moral and transcendent accomplishment.

Hsiaojen (小人) The Small-minded: Literally "small person," this term has been used in Confucian literature to indicate the mean-spirited person, the nitpicker. He is the opposite of the Gentleman, and a man of little virtue.

Tan (淡) The Light and Simple: This is one of the core concepts of Hung's philosophy. It is translated in the text variously as light, simple, weak-flavored, or plain, as determined by context or use in conjunction with other characters. Made up of the radicals for "fire" and "water," it would seem to mean washed out in color and taste. It can describe weak tea, thin wine, or a dinner of herbs. The Light and Simple hold the essence of existence.

Nung (濃) The Thick and Colorful: Also translated as the voluptuous and rich, it is the opposite of *tan*, a distraction from real living. It is used to describe bright colors and rich meats, and it has a connotation of the showy and gaudy.

Tanpeh (淡泊) Artlessness: This term can also be translated as simplicity, and it indicates the way one keeps his home or immediate surroundings, or his attitude. It is a positive quality unless it is overdone.

K'u (枯) Dried Up: Also translated as desiccated, withered, or elegantly simple, it is for Hung the *tanpeh* quality self-consciously pushed too far. Thus it lacks grace and humanity. Literally meaning a withered tree, the concept of *k'u* had appealed to the Taoists and Buddhists as a metaphor for the way the mind should be. By Hung's time its use had become somewhat hackneyed.

Ch'i (氣): The mysterious energy that runs through all things, from mountains to man to mind. *Ch'i* is a psycho-physical life force, and under certain circumstances should be controlled and directed. While never stating this explicitly in the text, Hung implies that *ch'i* is behind the vitality and positive tension of life, the results of controlled moderation and self-tempering.

Tao (道) The Way: The mysterious Tao, or Way of Life, is the underlying principle of all things. The Confucians have valued Tao as a social metaphor: The Way of Nature's model of proper Relationships—Heaven is superior to Earth, the planets do not stray from their orbits, the mountains are above and the rivers below. Thus it should be with human relationships. Hung agrees with this interpretation, but also uses the term in the more Taoist sense of the transcendent and spontaneous Principle of Life.

The Background

Hung Ying-ming lived toward the end of one of the most intellectually and spiritually stimulating times in Chinese history. Paradoxically, it was also one of the most stable periods, and one in which there was the least curiosity about anything that lay beyond China's borders.

The Ming Dynasty was established in 1368 by Chu Yuan-chang, an orphan and former Buddhist monk. Ending over a century and a half of Mongol domination, he established a dictatorial monarchy with direct management over the army, the bureaucracy, and the people, and he laid the foundation of a system so stable that it survived the fall of his dynasty in 1644 and lasted for another two hundred and fifty years.

Possibly because of their consciousness of former foreign control,[2] or perhaps because of the continuing harassment from the tribes to the north and the Japanese pirates along the eastern seaboard, the

Ming turned their focus inward, rebuilding most of the Great Wall and constructing a system of canals so that shipping could be conducted without exposure to the sea.

Social stability led to a growth in economic prosperity and accompanying advances in education, printing, and the availability of books. The rise in public education may have been a reflection of the first emperor's education as a well-versed Buddhist, but social thought was still predominantly the philosophy of Confucianism. Taoism, too, was featured in all levels of society, and not a few high governmental posts were filled by Taoist priests whose attitudes pervaded Ming official thought. Ch'an (Zen) Buddhism also resurged in popularity.

Contributing to the tendency toward syncretic thought was the great Confucian scholar-general Wang Yang-ming, who had studied Taoism as a young man, thereby adding to his understanding of Confucianism a meditative practice and vocabulary not dissimilar to Zen. His insistence that "knowledge and action are one," for example, was much closer to the Buddhist doctrine than Wang's Confucian peers were comfortable with.[3] Still, this doctrine spread throughout China and even as far as Japan.

Throughout the sixteenth century, the trend continued toward the unity of the "Three Creeds," culminating with the establishment of a "Three Creeds Church" in southeast China that was to have an influence on the direction of Chinese thought well into the eighteenth century. While the church itself was an extreme expression of this trend, there were many who were happy to be "eating off the one plate while eyeballing the other two"; and in general, the picture we get of the Ming mentality is a rejection of rigid orthodoxy and a cross-fertilization of views. Conversely, this reaffirmed the ancient Confucian concept of the natural equality of all men and all things in nature.

Each of the religions brought to this syncretic concept its own insights. The Confucians emphasized the social and moral metaphor that suggested itself, and the affirmation of life; the Buddhists found this a firm ground for the cultivation of and meditation on one's Original Nature; and the Taoists saw it as another way of explaining the Great Flow of Life. But the tendency was for a sort of unofficial agreement on man's oneness with nature, and the resulting mysticism permeated each group.

From this it was only a short step to the notion that sagehood was no longer an unattainable ideal belonging only to a few great men of the past. For if sagehood was now understood to be the formation of one body with Heaven and Earth and all things, it was certainly not out of reach for anyone here in the present. This ideal of a common humanity is the major thread that wends its way through Hung's *The Unencumbered Spirit.*

Hung Ying-ming and the Literati

With scholarship as active as it was during the Ming Dynasty, and China being the almost obsessively history-conscious country that it is, it is strange that we know so little about Hung Ying-ming, the author of the *The Unencumbered Spirit*. Yet he is mentioned in none of the eighty-nine volumes of Ming-Dynasty historical or biographical records, and most of what is believed to be true about him arose from conjecture and educated guesses. He is believed to have been the author of another book, the *Hsien-fo Ch'i-tsung* (*Marvelous Deeds of the Immortals and Buddhists*), which was supposedly completed in 1602. This work relates the sayings and deeds of the Taoist immortals, the Indian Buddhist patriarchs, and the Chinese patriarchs of Ch'an (Zen) Buddhism, and the mysteries of eternity. There is also a Buddhist tradition on Taiwan that Hung was the author of a number of other books, now lost: *Lien-chin* (*A String of Gems*),

Ch'iao-t'an (*Conversations with the Woodcutter*), *Pi-ch'ou* (*Fields Cleared by the Brush*), and *Ch'uan-chia Pao* (*Traditional House Treasures*), none of which sound particularly Confucian.

We come a little closer to the author through his friend or acquaintance Yu K'ung-chien, The Master of the Three Cliffs, who wrote the Prefatory Verse to *The Unencumbered Spirit* at the author's request. Yu does appear in the official records of the times, and through them we know that he had been a high official for twelve or thirteen years during the Wan-li period (1573–1619) before returning to private life after admonishing and then being ignored by the emperor Shen Tsung. Yu, however, was connected with the conservative Tung-lin Academy and was an associate of its founder, Ku Hsien-ch'eng.

This, along with the name, Hung Ying-ming,[4] is all the information we have apart from the book itself, which does not provide much in a definitive way. Hung does mention "our Confucianism," which scholars have jumped on to put him in the Confucian camp; and he mentions both his poverty and his association with nature. His connection with Yu K'ung-chien has given rise to speculation that his career may have run parallel to Yu's, but there is no documentary evidence of this. Could Hung have been Yu himself, writing under another name about his deeper and truer preoccupations?

A reading of the *The Unencumbered Spirit* reveals three things:

- First, Hung was a true Ming eclectic and a very heterodox thinker. He drew quite happily for inspiration from Confucianism, Taoism, and Zen Buddhism; and just as happily criticized them if their proponents or doctrines showed inconsistencies or wanderings from their central truths.

- Second, Hung must have been a well educated and widely read man. Often his writings are adaptations of, or contain allusions to, passages from Chinese literature spanning a period of over two millennia. These include philosophical works as diverse as the *Tao Te Ching*, the *Chuang Tzu*, the *Han Fei Tzu*, the *I Ching*, and the *Analects*; religious works such as the *Vimalakirti Sutra*, the *Diamond Sutra*, and the *Mumonkan*; and poets like Tao Yuan-ming, Po Chu-i, and Tu Fu, to name only a few.

- Third, as mentioned above, the author was likely the consummate member of the literati, or *wen-jen*, with an almost mystical concept of literature.

As mentioned earlier, concern with literature and what it means is nearly as old as Chinese civilization itself. The Chinese character that usually indicates literature, 文 (*wen*), as it appeared on Shang-Dynasty bronzes, seems to have originally meant "patterns," later referring specifically to patterns of nature and civilization, and then finally to writing itself. To the early Confucians it meant refinement and culture, and even embellishment. But by the third century of our era, writers such as Liu Hsieh and Liu Hsi[5] had developed a transcendent theory of literature, laying the foundation of both Chinese and Japanese literary thought for over a thousand years to come.

According to these men, the Tao, which is behind all natural principles and phenomena, manifests itself by patterns, 文. Thus, the waves and ripples of all bodies of water, the blooming and falling of flowers, the sounds of the wind, or the flight of birds are each a manifestation of the eternal principle for our contemplation. Man, too, has his patterns, which are filtered through his mind and are best expressed in literature, 文. If he will sit quietly and meditatively, they will naturally and spontaneously become manifest. In this way, there is an immediate connection between the patterns of the Tao and the purest patterns of man: Tao > Nature > Man > Literature. And the phrase "Literature is the vehicle of the Way" makes perfect sense. Stated specifically, "The way of Zen lies in intuitive apprehension [of Nature, or of our nature]; so does the way of poetry."[6] Indeed, this idea has traditionally worked both ways, and to this day Zen monks are often directed to meditate on certain poems rather than on Emptiness or the Tao.

Hung worked with this sense of pattern in both content and style—the former in the context of parallel metaphors or expressions, the latter in the patterns of his verses, which often use alternating numbers of Chinese characters to emphasize parallel meanings. In this translation, this is expressed in the line structure of the prose-poems themselves.

The Classics and the great poems, then, were not simply expressions of the Way; they were its very manifestations. And in this way the literati, by virtue of their contemplation of and participation in literature, and by their study of the universal patterns found in pursuits as varied as music, calligraphy, the drinking of tea, or the martial arts, were not mere dilettantes or escapists, but rather the men and women most in tune with the Tao and its underlying principles.

Such ideas, although never explained directly by Hung, run implicitly throughout his work. We can see in him the literary man of the Tao: a happy contemplative with his books and brushes and musical instruments, never far from nature or opposed to its pleasures. He was one of those attracted to the "lighter" sense of life he advocated in *The Unencumbered Spirit*. By combining a simple elegance with the ordinary, such men and women made their lives into artistic and poetic affairs. This sense, along with a particular understanding of Zen that makes an art of the simple in everyday life, has permeated Chinese and Japanese culture to the present day.

Acknowledgments

I first encountered *The Unencumbered Spirit* about forty years ago in a selection of translated verses from R. H. Blyth's *Haiku, Vol. 1*. Over the years I kept returning to this selection, and finally found that the book in its entirety was still very much in print. To my happy surprise, a door that had been only slightly ajar for so long was now open all the way.

There is, apparently, no original Chinese edition of *The Unencumbered Spirit* extant today. The various Chinese-Japanese editions currently available are based on two slightly differing Ming-Dynasty copies still preserved in Japan. I am particularly indebted to Imai Usaburo's *Saikontan*, especially for his notes on the literary references from which Hung worked, and for his clear exegesis of the text. Because of Imai's exhaustive scholarship, one is able to track down the sources of the original references and to work from them, rather than merely rely on translations into Japanese. I have included notes on those references that were often the wellspring of the author's musings, as well as on those that I felt were immediate and interesting or that are unavailable in English translation.

I am indebted to many people for their assistance in the completion of this text: to Prof. John Dreyer of the University of Miami, for his kind help with background material; to Homer D. Neal, the editor of the first edition of this project; to Barry Lancet, my current editor and literary guide; to John Siscoe, who has on more than one occasion helped me to wade through my own manuscripts; to Kate Barnes, Gary Haskins, Tom Levidiotis, Jim Brems, Daniel

Medvedov, Justin Newman, Jack Whisler, and many others for their encouragement and example; to my wife, Emily, for a patience beyond my understanding; and to my late professors, Hiraga Noburu and Richard McKinnon, from whom I was privileged to study for much too short a time.

Any and all mistakes are my own.

William Scott Wilson

NOTE ON *THE UNENCUMBERED SPIRIT* AND JAPAN

Although *The Unencumbered Spirit* was briefly enjoyed in China, it may well have not survived the conservative Confucian backlash of the Manchu Dynasty that occurred not long after its appearance. It has achieved its greatest popularity in Japan, where it was first printed in 1822 and has continued to be republished in new editions regularly. The reason for this is, perhaps, not hard to understand.

Since ancient times the Japanese have believed in the efficacy of *kotodama*, the soul and spirit of words, not only to cleanse human beings, but to affect the gods themselves. By the early sixth or seventh centuries A.D., prayers called *norito* were collected by Shinto priests to be recited for such purposes, and one can still visit a large Shinto shrine today to find farmers or businessmen repeating these prayers aloud in emotional trances of supplication. This belief in the power of words was confirmed by Ki no Tsurayuki in the early tenth century, when he wrote in his introduction to the *Kokinshu*, the first imperial anthology of poetry:

> Without particular effort, it is poetry that moves Heaven and Earth, makes the unseen gods and demons feel sympathy, brings harmony to the relations of man and woman, and softens the hearts of rough warriors.

Thus, prayer, poetry, and to a certain extent magic had unclear boundaries in ancient Japan, and indeed, in early times, poets and priests were held in similar esteem.

In the late fourteenth and early fifteenth centuries, this attention to *kotodama* was used in yet a different genre by Zeami Motokiyo, the father of the classical Japanese drama Noh. His plays, written in part with the same rhythmic double-lined arrangements as *norito*, still seem to have the same therapeutic effect on spectators—both human, and possibly divine—today as they did in his time.

Adding still another dimension to this mystical concept of words and their arrangements was the appearance of the literati (文人) in Japan in the seventeenth and eighteenth centuries. Like their Chinese counterparts, such men and women—mostly painters, poets, musicians, and even martial artists—paid special attention to the patterns of the natural world around them and applied them to their own lives and arts. This, in combination with a rekindling of interest in the *I Ching* throughout the Tokugawa period, set the stage for a book of meditations on the patterns of human existence that could be recited or even chanted.

Finally, the *Ts'ai Ken T'an* is a book that celebrates a diversity of religious and philosophical outlooks. Thus, it should be no surprise that the Japanese, who are traditionally married in a Shinto ceremony, given death rites and posthumous names by Buddhist priests, and conduct their worldly affairs with a high Confucian code, have found a deep and lasting resonance in its every line.

The Unencumbered Spirit

Confucius, the Buddha, and Lao Tzu are depicted in this detail of a fifteenth-century painting entitled *The Patriarchs of the Three Creeds*, attributed to Josetsu, considered the father of Zen ink painting. See the Afterword for further discussion. (Courtesy of Kenninji, Ryosoku-in Collection, Kyoto.)

A PREFATORY VERSE

Refusing visitors, making my own tracks,
    living alone in my thatched hut;
Enjoying the company of those living in the Way,
    but taking no pleasure in the company of those who bypass it.

Arguing without restraint with past philosophers and sages
    about the similarities and differences
    among the Confucian Five Books;[1]
But enough at leisure to roam around with two or three disciples
    at the foot of the ever-changing mountains and clouds.

Singing and chanting every day
    with the fishermen and farmers on the beaches of the Five Lakes,
    or in the hollows of the green fields,
But rarely expressing myself or mixing
    with those in places of fickle passions or arenas of carnage, who compete for trifles and who consider the insignificant as prosperity.

Occasionally, those learning the Sung philosophy
    I would nurture;
Those learning the Law of the Buddha,
    I would enlighten.

But the simple chatterboxes and loudmouths,
    I would send on their way.

This should be sufficient to indicate my capability
    for living in the mountains.

At one point my friend, Hung Ying-ming,
    brought his book to show me,
    and asked me to write a preface.
Finally I straightened up the old books on my desk,
    swept away worldly thoughts from my breast,
    took it in hand, and understood:

When he discusses Original Character,
    I enter directly into its essence;
When he speaks of human nature,
    I exhaust its inner workings in every way.
By his actions between Heaven and Earth,
    I see the gentle waves within his breast.

Achievement and fame he regards as dust and waste,
    and I immediately grasp the loftiness of his insights.
The accomplishment of his brush
    is never far from green trees and blue mountains,
And the craft of his words
    is in the flight of hawks and the leaping of fish.

To what extent this man is enlightened
    I am naturally unable to provide deep proof.
But based on the words he has strewn,
    which are a warning to the world

and essential to awakening men,
This is not simply a display that enters the ears
and leaves through the mouth.

He names these discussions "Vegetable Root."
They have come originally from the midst of integrity
and discipline, and have been culled from the core
of cultivation and care.

One can imagine that
he has tumbled and fallen in the wind and the waves,
been harassed and harried along steep cliffs.

Master Hung says in these pages,
"If Fate sends toil and thus affects my body,
I put my mind at peace and assist myself in this way.
If Fate brings obstructions and thus affects my circumstances,
I elevate my Way and pass along with ease."[2]

One gets the impression
of his discretion and of a strength he can call his own.
And so, with these several words I introduce this work
and make it public to all—
One should know that true taste
Lies within the vegetable root.

The Master of Three Cliffs,
Yu K'ung-chien

BOOK ONE

1.

If you strive to make Truth your home,
You may sometimes be lonely;
But fawning on the powerful and influential,
You will feel the chill of solitude for the ages.

2.

When you step but lightly through the world,
You are but lightly affected by it;
But when you pass through events with a deeper tread,
Their tricks and schemes are profound.[1]
Thus the gentleman knows
Simplicity is better than a show of dexterity.
Thus he knows
A rude single-mindedness is better than a distorted show of manners.

3.

The gentleman's disposition
Is like the clear sky, the bright sun,
And he should not hide it from others.
The gentleman's outstanding abilities

Are like concealed jewels or gems stored away:[2]
He should not easily reveal them.

4.

Those with power, fame, wealth, and extravagance—
By not coming close to them a man stays pure.
Yet the man who can approach and not be affected
is the purest of all.
Those who are clever, artful, and full of guile[3]—
By not knowing them a man stays high-minded.
Yet the man who can know and still not use them
is the most high-minded of all.

5.

Our ears forever hear things distasteful to them.[4]
Our mind is forever filled with events contrary to
our desires.
But such situations are exactly the whetstones for
advancing our virtue, for putting our discipline into
practice.
If we always heard words pleasing to our ears,
Living this life would be just like being buried
alive in poison.

6.

When winds grow bitter and rains angry,
Even small birds are frightened and sad.
When skies become clear and breezes are bright,
The grasses and trees are fresh and full of joy.
From this it can be seen that
　Heaven and Earth are unable to go one day without
　　harmony;
　The human heart is unable to go one day without joy.

7.

Strong wines and fatty meats, sweets and spicy foods—
　These do not possess true taste.
True taste is only found in the light and simple.
The mysterious and strange, the preeminent and
　　uncommon—
　These are not the man who has arrived.[5]
The man who has arrived is only the ordinary man.

8.

Heaven and Earth remain peacefully unmoved,
Yet their life-breath is unceasing, and seldom rests.[6]
The sun and moon hasten through their courses day and
night,
Yet their constant light has not changed through the ages.[7]
Thus for the gentleman,
It is necessary during times of leisure
to keep in mind what is proper for emergencies.
It is necessary during times of haste
to retain an element of composure.

9.

Late at night, when others are at rest,
Sitting alone, I look deep into my heart:
For the first time, distractions cease, and the truth alone
becomes manifest, as dew appears at dawn.
At such times
I experience a free and responsive mind.
Now the truth is manifested about the past, and I am
once again aware of how difficult it is to escape
distractions.
At such times
I experience mortification and shame.

10.

Injury can appear in the midst of kindness.[8]
When happy, keep your wits about you.
The aftermath of failure can be turned into success.
When things don't go the way you want,
Do not be quick to give up the ghost.

11.

Of those who make their meals from simple herbs and vegetables, their repasts are as pure as ice, as stainless as gems.
Of those who dress in fancy clothes and feast sumptuously, they lower themselves to acting like servants and slaves.
Ultimately the will is made clear by simplicity,
And integrity lost by opulence.

12.

Your attitude while still in the world
Should be open and free,
saving others from the grief of discontent.
The benefits you leave after you are gone
Should flow the length of time,
steeping others in feelings of ease.

13.

When walking narrow pathways,[9]
Step back a pace, let your companion go ahead.
When eating delicious rich foods,
Surrender one-third of your portion for others to enjoy.
  This is the law for making your way
    most comfortably through the world.

14.

In becoming a person of merit, though you perform no
    lofty deeds,
  If you are able to shake off mundane concerns,
  You will become one of the renowned.
In pursuing studies, though you make no claim to ingenuity,
  If you are able to decrease externals that afflict the
    heart,[10]
  You will cross over to the land of the sages.

15.

Associating with friends, you should show some chivalry.
Laying up merit, you need at least a modicum of the
artless.[11]

16.

Avoid putting your own blessings and profits before
others,
But do not fall behind them in moral progress.
When receiving, do not go beyond your share,
But when conducting yourself in a course of action,
do not do less than you should.

17.

In passing through this world,
one is esteemed if he steps back
a pace for others to go ahead.
Stepping backward is thus
Preliminary[12] to stepping forward.
In serving others, it is felicitous to show
a bit of magnanimity.
Benefiting others is truly
The foundation of benefiting yourself.

18.

Even if you have performed world-shaking meritorious deeds,[13]
If pride is involved then the value is lost.
Even if you have committed a crime that has reached the heavens,
If you have truly repented, regret will find no home.

19.

Fame and honor—
These are not things you should assume only for yourself.
If you divide these up and confer them on others,
You will be able to keep harm at a distance and make yourself replete.
Disgraceful conduct and ill repute—
These are not things you should thrust onto others.
If you will lighten others' burdens and ascribe them to yourself,
You will be able to veil your own brilliance and cultivate virtue.

20.

No matter what you do,
    If you forsake ideas of excess and inexhaustibility
    The Creator of Things will be unable to scorn you,[14]
    And the gods and spirits will be unable to do you harm.
If you invariably seek satisfaction in your own undertakings,
Or habitually seek for your own efforts to be fulfilled,[15]
If some calamity does not occur internally,
    You will surely invite sorrow from without.

21.

In every household there is a true Buddha;
In everyday life you will find true men of the Way.
If a man can be sincere in his heart, harmonious in spirit,
    Joyful in countenance and pleasant in his words,
    If he will serve his parents and siblings,
    Laying aside reserve in body and spirit,
    Letting his temperament flow with those around him,
Such a man will be far superior to those who regulate their breathing or practice meditation.

22.

Those who love activity are like lightning seen through
clouds or lanterns flickering in the wind.
Those who practice quietism are like dead ashes[16]
or withered trees.
One should be like the hawk that flies, the fish that leaps
in still waters.[17]
By this, one enters the mind and the body of the Way.

23.

When attacking someone's faults
Do not be too severe.
You need to consider how well he will weather what he
hears.
When teaching someone by showing him what is good,
Do not pass certain heights,
But hit upon what he should be able to follow.

24.

The vermin that crawl through the dung are the extremity
of filth,
But transformed they become cicadas drinking dew
in the autumn wind.
Rotten grass has no light,
But it metamorphoses and becomes the fireflies that
shine with iridescence under the summer moon.
Know this well:
The pure always comes from that which is stained;
The bright is forever born from the totally dark.

25.

Lofty pride, haughty arrogance—
These are nothing more than rashness and false courage.
When you have been able to bring this rashness under
submission,
Then the right mind will grow.
Carnal passions and calculations of gain and loss—
These are but attachments of the confused mind.
When the confused mind has been totally
extinguished,
Then the true mind will appear.

26.

When you think of food after filling your stomach,
The boundary between the flavorful and the insipid
disappears completely.
When you think of sex after a liaison,
The [true] attraction between man and woman totally
melts away.
Thus, if you always think of the remorse that follows
the act
And thwart the foolish confusion that comes with
facing the situation,
Your disposition will be composed, your actions not
incorrect.

27.

When outfitted in the accouterments of a high official,
You should still relish the mountain recluse.
When living among the forests and springs,
You should preserve in your heart the administration of
the state.[18]

28.

Living in the world is not necessarily a matter of waiting
eagerly for every chance to perform a meritorious
deed.
Making no mistakes is in itself a meritorious deed.
Interacting with people is not a matter of seeking others
to feel gratitude for your own virtue.
Not earning their hostility is in itself a virtue.

29.

To be overly concerned about your duties is a beautiful
virtue,
But to bring yourself too much hardship because of them
is neither fitting to your constitution
nor felicitous to human nature.
To revere simplicity and be unattached is indeed an
indication of high character,
But to maintain too much elegant simplicity is
neither helpful to mankind
nor useful to the world at large.

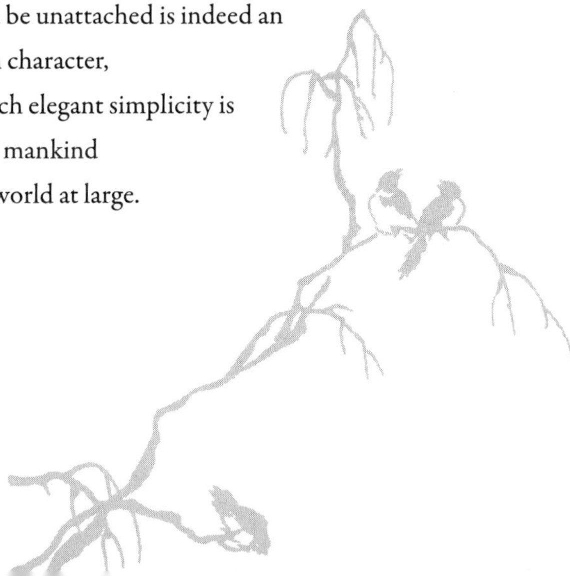

30.

When your work has come to a standstill and you can
neither advance nor retreat,
You should relocate the mentality with which you began.[19]
When your efforts have been realized and your actions
are fulfilled,
You need to look carefully farther down the road.

31.

People of wealth and status—
They should possess kindness and large-heartedness;
Far too often, they are envious and unsympathetic.
They are bathed with wealth and status, yet practice
poverty and penny-pinching.
How will they ever gain true wealth?
People both clever and intelligent—
They should keep their abilities concealed, in reserve;
Far too often, they place their talent on bright display.
They are blessed with cleverness and intelligence, yet are
possessed of folly and sightlessness.
How will they not be defeated?

32.

After you have resided in a lowly position,
You know the danger of climbing to a high status.
After you have been in shadow and darkness,
You know the great exposure of facing the bright and clear.
After you have abided in inactivity,[20]
You know the overexertion of those who love activity.
After you cultivated yourself with silence,
You know the confusion of an abundance of words.

33.

Release the mind that desires merit and fame, wealth and distinction,
And you will be able to avoid the ordinary.
Release the mind that desires the Way and its virtue, humanity and righteousness,[21]
And you will, for the first time, be able to join the sages.

34.

Although the desire for gain will not completely damage the mind,

Egoistic opinion is a cutworm and will inevitably eat it away.

Although women and song will not necessarily keep you from the Way,

Intellect and cleverness raise a barrier and will shut you out in the end.

35.

The human heart will reverse itself.

The road through this world is steep and uphill.

For places that are difficult to pass

You should know the law of stepping back a pace for others.

For places that are easily traveled,

You should give some breathing space to others, so they may do the same.

36.

When dealing with people of no status,

It is easy to be severe,

But difficult not to be hateful.

When dealing with people of high status,

It is easy to be fawning,

But difficult to maintain proper decorum.

37.

Better to abide in simplicity and repel cleverness,
To retain a bit of right-mindedness,
To return to Heaven and Earth.
Better to decline the overly gorgeous and to content yourself with artlessness,
To bequeath one pure name,
To remain in Heaven and Earth.

38.

If you would quell demons,
You must first subjugate your own mind.[22]
When the mind has yielded, then the legions of demons will disperse obediently.
If you would drive away deceitfulness,
You must first bridle your own spirit.
When your spirit is at peace, heresies will not bother you.

39.

Teaching a disciple is like bringing up a well-protected maiden:
It is absolutely necessary to be strict about coming and going, and to be cautious about friends and associates.

If a person becomes intimate with noxious people even
once,
This is sowing one impure seed in an unsullied field.
Then it will be difficult, throughout a lifetime, to have
even one unblighted seedling.

40.

On the road of desire, do not happily dip your fingers
into the pot just because it happens to be there.
Once you have stuck them in and tasted what is inside,
You will try to put them in ten thousand fathoms deep.
On the road of principle, do not step back even a little,
hesitating over the difficulties.
Once you have stepped back in retreat,
You will be separated from your goal by a thousand
mountains.

41.

One whose disposition is conscientious will be attentive
toward himself, attentive toward others.
He will be attentive in all things.
One whose disposition is indifferent will be unreserved
toward himself, unreserved toward others.
He will be unreserved in all affairs.
Therefore, the gentleman,
In all those things for which he habitually has a taste,
Should not lean toward the overly gorgeous.
Neither should he incline toward the elegantly simple.

42.

If others possess wealth, then I possess humanity;
If others possess high status, then I possess justice.
Therefore, the gentleman never forces his thoughts on
others.
If men would be persistent, they could gain mastery of
Heaven;
If they concentrated their wills, they would have
command of their *ch'i*.[23]
The gentleman does not accept
the shackles of the created world.

43.

In establishing yourself in life,
if you do not raise yourself at least one step higher,
It will be like shaking off your clothes in a dust cloud,
Like washing your feet in the mud.
How will you ever excel?
In living with the world, if you do not step back a single pace for others,
You will be like the moth that hurls itself into the lamp,
Or the ram that catches its horns in the hedge.[24]
How will you ever be at peace?

44.

If you want to study, it is necessary to collect your spirit,
And to concentrate in earnest.
But if in cultivating virtue there remains any idea of merit or fame,
Learning will inevitably amount to nothing.
And if in reading books you have a tendency toward recitation and stylishness,
Surely there will nothing in the depths of your heart.

45.

All men have the capacity for great benevolence:
The mind of the Bodhisattva Vimalakirti is no different
than that of a butcher or executioner.
All places have the capacity for true pleasure:
A house made of gold is no different
than a hut with thatched eaves.
Ah, but desire creeps in and passion envelopes,
And that which is right in front of you is mixed and
mistaken,
Causing the tiniest fraction of an inch to become a
thousand miles.

46.

In improving your worth or in practicing the Way,
It is necessary to have a mind as unmoving as trees and
stones.
Having once become envious or elated,
You will skip along to the world of desire.
In benefiting society or participating in government,
It is necessary to have an attitude as free flowing as
water and clouds.
Once you covet or become attached,
You will fall crashing into crisis and extremity.

47.

It is a matter of course that the daily behavior of good men
is tranquil and propitious.
Thus their sleep and dreams, their spirits and souls
Are never without peace.
It is a matter of course that the daily actions of bad men
are brutish and frightening.
Thus the sounds of their words and laughter
Are all transfused with malevolence.

48.

When the liver ails, it will soon follow
That the eye is unable to focus.
When the kidney is afflicted, it will soon follow
That the ear is unable to distinguish sounds.
Illness begins in a place unseen by men,
But invariably develops to a condition
that can be seen by all.
Therefore, the gentleman,
If he hopes not to be censored in the light of day,
Commits no crimes in secret.

49.

There is no happiness like the happiness of having few
affairs.
There is no misfortune like that of having many worries.
Only the man who is troubled with affairs
ultimately knows the happiness having few affairs
brings.
Only the man whose mind is at peace
gets to know the misfortune having many worries
entails.

50.

When living in a time of order, one should act with
propriety.[25]
When living in a time of confusion, one should adapt to
circumstances.[26]
In these degenerate days
It is best to act in both ways.
When dealing with good men, one should be
magnanimous.
When dealing with bad men, one should be strict.
In commerce with the ordinary run of men,
It is best to be both harmoniously.

51.

You should forget the service you have rendered to others,
    But not the troubles you have caused.
You should not forget the favors others have done for you,
    But discard feelings of enmity.

52.

When doing a favor,
    If inwardly you put no value on your own action
    And outwardly do not calculate the feelings of the other,
Then a spoonful of grain will equal the blessings of a hundred bushels.
When your actions benefit another,
    If you measure your own charity
    And press the other for recompense,
Then a thousand in payment have scarcely the merit of a few coins.

53.

Among the circumstances in which people find themselves,
Some are satisfactory and others are not.
How can you want only your own to be replete?
As for the workings of your heart,
It is at some times in order and at other times not.
How can you expect the heart of others to be always so
constant?
Look deeply into relativity and harmonize things
accordingly.
This will be a convenient way to the gate of truth.

54.

Having purified your mind,
read books and study the ancients.
If you do not study in this way,
When you see a good act,
You'll purloin it to make yourself look good.
Hearing a good word,
You'll borrow it to cover your own shortcomings.
This is lending weapons to the enemy
And bringing food to the thief.

55.

The prideful live rich lives but are not satisfied.
How can they equal the frugal man who lives as a pauper
but has a surplus?
The able exert themselves but reap the hostility of others.
How can they equal the inept man who lives in idleness
but consummates Truth?[27]

56.

Reading books but not seeing the wisdom and
intelligence within—
This is being a slave to paper and print.
Being of high rank but not loving the people—
This is a thief wearing ceremonial robes.
Lecturing on learned subjects but not giving proper
respect to putting them into action—
This is Zen of the mouth alone.
Performing great achievements but giving no thought
to the seeds of virtue for the future—
This is only flowers blooming and withering right
before your eyes.

57.

In every human heart there is one volume of the Book of
Truth.
But all is packed away on the shelves,
Pages here and pages there.
In every human heart there is one score for the Music of
Veracity.
But all is buried under
Popular songs and glamorous dances.
The person who studies should sweep away externals
And immediately seek what has been there from the
beginning.
Only then will he be able to put this truth to use.

58.

In the midst of painstaking labor,
There is always a way to make the heart glad.
At the time of one's prosperity,
The sorrow of disappointment may quickly be born.

59.

Riches and status, fame and honor—
Those who come from morality and principle
Are like flowers in mountain forests:
  Of their own they gently spread and grow.
Those who come from work and effort
Are like the flowers in pots and trays:
  They can be put in or taken out, planted or thrown
    away.
Those who gained by power and influence,
Are like flowers stuck in a vase or jar:
  As their roots are not planted,
  They will fade and wilt in no time at all.

60.

When spring comes, the season softens:
  The flowers spread thickly in colors more beautiful;
  The birds sing continuously verses lovely of sound.
The person of rank happily stands out from the crowd,
For all to see, well fed and well dressed.
But if he does not aspire to compose beautiful verses,
    to perform good deeds,
Though he lives for one hundred years
He will never have truly lived for a single day.

61.

The student of the Way keeps his thoughts
circumspect and discreet,
But needs also a penchant for the clean and refined.
Yet if he only brings himself under earnest control,
making himself pure and impecunious,
It will be the killing of autumn, not the birth of spring.
How will he give growth to the Ten Thousand
Things?[28]

62.

True purity contains no fame within;
He who establishes a reputation for himself does so
strictly out of desire.
Great skill[29] contains no art within;
He who mindfully uses technique does so only out of
clumsiness.

63.

When the water bottle is full, it overturns.[30]
While the piggy bank remains empty, it is whole.
Therefore, the gentleman
Resides in vacuity rather than existence,
And exists in the lacking rather than the complete.

64.

If you have not yet uprooted the desire for fame,
    Though you belittle the command of a thousand chariots,
    And content yourself with only a gourd from which to drink[31]—
This is still crashing into the dusty passions of the world.
If you have not yet tempered your own hot-bloodedness,
    Though you benefit amply from within the four seas
    And rake in profit from the entire world—
This is, in the end, nothing but a show.

65.

When the true mind is bright and shiny,
    You will have fair weather even in a dark room.
When your thoughts are dark and gloomy,
    Evil demons will be born even under a bright sun.

66.

Men know the happiness of fame and position.
They do not know that obscurity and lack of position
  Is the happiness of the highest truth.
Men know the affliction of hunger and cold.
They do not know that being rid of hunger or cold
  Is an affliction more excessive still.

67.

Those who do evil and yet fear that men should learn of it
  Are, in the midst of evil, still on the road to good.
Those who do good and yet want that men should soon
    learn of it
  Live within the good, but are truly at nothing other
    than the foot of iniquity.

68.

The contrivances of Heaven are unfathomable:
  They are repressed, and then increase;
  They increase, and then are repressed.
In all, they make sport of heroes,
And set great men on their heads.

Thus, if reverses come to the gentleman, he receives them as routine.
When living at peace, he thinks of the emergency,[32]
And Heaven has no place to use its skills.

69.

The man with an arid personality surges like fire:
Whatever he chances into, he burns.
The man with little sense of kindness is as cold as pure ice:
Whatever encounters him is killed off for sure.
The man who is stagnant and clinging[33] is like dead water or rotten wood:
His life-force is already cut off.
With any of these it will be difficult
To establish good works or prolong the good life.

70.

Happiness[34] cannot be sought: nourish your own spirit of joy.
This alone is the foundation for beckoning happiness.
Disaster cannot be avoided: flee from that which encourages brutality.
This alone is the way to avoid disaster's reach.

71.

Of the things we say, nine out of ten hit the mark;
Yet we do not necessarily count this as strange.
But let one word miss the mark, and people will line up to complain.[35]
Of the things we plan, nine out of ten come to pass;
Yet we do not necessarily ascribe this to our due.
But let one plan go awry, and people will crowd in to revile.
For this reason, the gentleman
Remains silent rather than makes noise;
Shows ineptitude rather than displays a skill.

72.

When the breath of Heaven and Earth is warm, there is birth;
When it is cold, there is death.
Therefore, he whose nature is indifferent
Receives blessings that are less than lukewarm.
Only the man of friendly spirit and warm heart[36]
Will have fortune that is also kind
And blessings that are long-lived.

73.

The road to the Principle of Heaven is extremely
abundant.
If you divert your mind there for but a little way,[37]
You will feel in your breast both vastness and light.
The road of human desire is extremely restricted.
If you approach it by only a step,
Wherever you look will be brambles and mire.

74.

When you train yourself with both suffering and joy,
Ah, what blessings come when this training is taken to
the extreme:
They are, for the first time, blessings that last.
When you think things through with both doubt and
faith,
The knowledge that comes when this thinking is taken
to the extreme
Is, for the first time, a knowledge of truth.

75.

The mind should always be void,[38]
For once void, Justice and Principle may enter and reside.
The mind may not be without Truth,
For once Truth is there, desire will not enter in.

76.

Where the earth has been neglected, many things grow.
Where the water is clear, there are never any fish.[39]
Therefore, the gentleman
Should be acquainted to an extent with embracing impurity and accepting stain.[40]
He should not hold onto the total chastity of only loving the pure and going his own way.

77.

The restive horse that has overturned the carriage
Can, at last, be made to run properly.
The melting metal that leaps out of the mold
Can, at last, be returned to the cast.[41]
But the man who lives only in peaceful amusement without arousing himself to action
Will, until the end of his life, make no progress at all.
Pai-sha[42] said,

"There are many ailments involved in becoming a man,
But none are sufficient to make him hide his face in
shame.
I lament only the man who lives his life without any
ailment at all."
This is truly a solid argument.

78.

Man, with simply one thought of greed,
Will melt away his strength and transform it into
weakness,
Will obstruct his wisdom and create ignorance,
Will change kindness into cruelty,
Will stain the pure and produce the tarnished,
And so will completely destroy the character of his entire
life.
Therefore, the ancients
Considered the lack of greed to be a gem,
And thus did they transcend the everyday world.

79.

Ears, eyes, seeing, hearing—these are the thieves of the
external.
Emotion, desire, consciousness of self—these are the
thieves of the internal.
Only when the Old Man who is master,[43]
Bright of mind and unobscured by desire,
Sits alone within the temple,
Will the thieves be transformed into servants of the
House.

80.

Instead of making plans for works that have not yet been
completed,
You should preserve the projects that have already been
achieved.
Instead of regretting the mistakes of the past,
You should hold in check your crimes of the future.

81.

Our disposition should be lofty and broad,
    But not to the point of being distant and abstracted.
Our thoughts should be detailed and conscientious,
    But not to the point of being tedious and nit-picking.
Our tastes should be simple and ascetic,
    But not to the point of eccentricity and desiccation.
Our virtue should be strict and clear-cut,
    But not to the point of vehemence or rage.

82.

The wind soughs through the bamboo,
And when it has passed,
        the bamboo has no sound.
The geese fly over the cold clear pool,[44]
And when they have gone,
        the pool retains no image.
Therefore, for the gentleman,
    A thing is manifest when it appears
        for the first time in his mind;
    When the thing has ceased,
        his mind commits itself
        to the void.

83.

Being pure and yet tolerant,
Being warmhearted and yet resolved,
Having insight but not speculating on the faults of others,
Being upright but not beyond reform—
All of these can be called honeyed biscuits, not too sweet;
Or products of the sea, not too salty.
Only this is balanced virtue.

84.

Even an impoverished house may have its grounds swept clean;
Even a penniless woman may comb her hair neatly.
Though what is seen may not be enticingly beautiful,
The grace within is refined of its own accord.
Even the gentleman of rank may for a time encounter suffering and ruin.
But will he let himself suffer neglect each time this occurs?

85.

If you do not pass time thoughtlessly when at leisure,
It will stand you in good stead when you are busy.
If you do not sit there blankly when at peace,
It will stand you in good stead when you are active.
If you do not deceive others when you are unobserved,
It will stand you in good stead when you are clearly seen.

86.

When the mind is aroused,
As soon as you become aware that it has taken the road of desire,
Force it aside and lead it back to the road of principle.
When the mind is aroused, you become aware.
When you become aware, you can make changes.
This is precisely the time
To change disaster into fortune,
To raise the dead and bring them back to life.
Never let such times pass lightly by.

87.

When your thoughts are at peace and have become transparent,
You see the true form of the mind.
When your feelings are at rest and have become tranquil,
You understand the true movements of the mind.
When your disposition is disinterested and totally calm,
You obtain the true flavor of the mind.
There is nothing that can rival these three.

88.

The peace that comes from peaceful surroundings is not true peace.
Only in the peace obtained in the midst of activity
Is found the true sphere of one's original nature.
The pleasure that comes from pleasurable surroundings is not true pleasure.
Only with the pleasure obtained in the midst of suffering
Can one see the true movements of the mind.

89.

In sacrificing yourself for others, let there be no doubt in your actions.
If doubt resides there, in the very will to make the sacrifice
There will be much shame.
In rendering services to others, do not seek compensation.
If compensation is sought,
It will equal the mentality of your sacrifice:
Both are at fault.

90.

If Fate is stingy with me and thus affects my fortune,
I make my virtue ample, and greet my fortune in this way.
If Fate sends toil and thus affects my body,
I put my mind at peace and assist myself in this way.
If Fate brings obstructions and thus affects my circumstances,
I make my Way and pass along with ease.
More than this, what can Fate do with me?

91.

In his heart, a man of principle does not wait in
anticipation of good fortune.
Heaven attaches itself to this mind of no anticipation,
and guides his sincerity.
The crafty man maintains his determination to avoid
disaster.
Heaven abides in the midst of this attachment to
determination, and harasses his soul.
Thus we can see that
The workings of Heaven are the greatest mystery,
But the wisdom and art of man are of questionable
gain.

92.

If the song-and-dance girl latches onto a good man
in her later years,
The rouge and flowers of her former life will be no
obstacle at all.
If the chaste wife lets down her guard after her gray hairs
have begun to show,
The purity and work of half a life together come to
naught.

The proverb says,
    "In scanning the life of a man, look only at the latter
        half of his years."[45]
This is truly a wise saying.

93.

If a common person ventures to cultivate virtue
        or perform a good deed,
It is just like being a high official, but without rank.
If a man of high rank uselessly indulges in his power
        or markets his position,
He becomes, in the end, only a titled beggar.

94.

If you would ask about the blessing[46] left by your ancestors,
It is the very life you have received.
    You should think of the accumulation of troubles[47]
        they had.
If you would ask about the benefits you will leave to your
        descendents,
It is what your life will leave behind.
    You must think of how easy that is to turn upside down.

95.

The gentleman who pretends to be good
    Is no different from the scoundrel who commits evil at
        will.
The gentleman who falls from honor
    Does not measure up to the villain who improves his
        intent.

96.

When a friend or relative makes a mistake,
    It is best not to become violently angry,
    But nor should you neglect it.
If the affair is difficult to discuss,
    Give the subject a different tact;
    Hide the one, suggest the other.
If today he does not understand,
    Patiently await another time, and admonish him again.
Be like the spring winds that thaw the frozen ground;
Be like the soft *ch'i* that melts away the ice.
    Only with this will you be a model to your family.

97.

If your mind always assumes a peaceful state,
The world will not seem lacking,

If your mind forever frees itself by practicing tolerance
    and impartiality,
The world will show no distortion in human nature.

98.

The man who takes things lightly
  Will necessarily be doubted by those of a more
    obstinate disposition.
A man both strict and severe
  Will many times be loathed by those more self-
    indulgent.
The gentleman places himself in these situations
And should neither change from his former integrity
Nor be too revealing of his own skills.

99.

In the midst of reverses,
  All around you are acupuncture needles and medicine
  To polish your integrity or burnish your behavior.
Yet, you remain unaware of these.
Circumscribed by favorable events,
  Arrayed in front of you are battle swords, halberds,
    and spears
  To melt away the fat and whittle away your bones.
Yet, of these, too, you remain unaware.

100.

A person brought up closely surrounded by wealth and rank
Will have appetites like raging fires
And wield power like violent flames.
If he cannot become cool and clear,
If his flames do not actually burn someone else,
They will surely scorch the man himself.

101.

When the human heart has sincerity,
It can drive away the frost,
Can cause battlements to fall,
And penetrate metal and stone.[48]
But if a man lives with deception,
Though his body may be replete in its vanity,
The true master,[49] his soul, will have perished.
When in the company of men, his countenance will be reviled;
When by himself, his own form and shadow will be
Embarrassments to themselves.

102.

When literature is taken to its highest level,
There is nothing particularly extraordinary about it:
    It is simply appropriate.
When human character is developed to its fullest,
There is nothing particularly wonderful about it:
    It is simply natural.

103.

If we speak of the world of illusion,
Then merit, fame, riches, and status,
    Not to mention our very limbs and bodies, are all
        attached to the form entrusted to us.[50]
If we speak of the world of truth,
Then father, mother, brothers, and sisters,
    Not to mention the rest of creation,[51] are all of one
        body with us.

If a man is able to see through these things
And recognize the truth,
    Only then will he be capable of taking responsibility
        for the world's encumbrances,
    Only then will he be capable of stripping off society's
        chains.[52]

104.

Those things pleasant to the taste[53]
Are all poisons;[54] they inflame the intestines and rot the bones.
If you will halve your portions, you should find no divine reproach.
Those things pleasurable to the mind
Are all go-betweens; they break down abilities and eradicate virtue.
If you will halve your portions, you should be without regret.

105.

Do not attack men's smaller mistakes.
Do not expose men's private affairs.
Do not think of men's former crimes.[55]
With these three,
You can nourish your virtue and keep harm at a distance.

106.

The gentleman of rank should not take his conduct
lightly.
Taking it lightly, he will be easily bent by the world
around him,
And will never have the likelihood of leisure or peace.
He should not take his mind's workings so solemnly.
For taking them seriously, the world will stick to him like
mud,
And his actions will be neither lively nor refined.

107.

Heaven and Earth exist for ten thousand ages,
But this body you will not receive again.
Man's life spans no more than a hundred years,
But the days pass with the greatest of ease.
You who have had the good fortune to be born
Should not be unknowing of the joy of existence,
Nor yet free in your breast of the sorrow of life's vanity.

108.

When favors exist, hostility completes the pattern.[56]
Thus, rather than make others feel that you have bestowed favors,
You should forget both favor and hostility.
When mercy exists, enmity is aroused.
Thus, rather than make others feel that you have been merciful,
You should annihilate both mercy and enmity.

109.

The diseases of old age
Are all incurred at the time of our youth.[57]
The adversities[58] that overtake us as we start to decline
Were all created at the time of our prosperity.
Therefore, the gentleman is apprehensive
When handling an overflow of wealth
Or treading the road of the replete.[59]

110.

Rather than marketing personal favors,
contribute to public opinion.
Rather than making bonds with new acquaintances,
be cordial with old friends.

Rather than establishing a shining reputation,
sow secret acts of virtue.[60]
Rather than admiring the extraordinarily virtuous,
respect ordinary behavior.

111.

Correct and impartial views—you should not set your hand to violate these.
Once violated, your shame will remain ten thousand generations.
Places of authority, gatherings for profit—you should not set a foot inside.
With a single step inside, your whole life will be blemished.

112.

Rather than distorting your own beliefs to make others happy,
Make yourself correct and make others mad.
Rather than rendering no good and receiving others' praise,
Commit no evil and obtain their slander.

113.

When disaster has come to a father, brother, or other blood relative,
Compose yourself properly, and do not become rattled.
When you encounter the faults of a friend or associate,
Act appropriately and do not hesitate or delay.

114.

Do not be careless with small leaks,
Do not deceive in the dark,
Do not become lazy and neglectful at the end of the road.
Only with these three will you become exalted.

115.

Even with a thousand in cash it is difficult to tie down more than a moment of happiness.
Surprisingly, even a single meal[61] will render a person grateful for the rest of his life.
For ultimately, when love is too ponderous, it creates its opposite, aversion.
But when light, love reverses again, and engenders joy.

116.

Hide your skill under a show of inability:[62]
    Display dim-wittedness, but continue to be bright;[63]
    Let your purity reside within the muddy;
    By means of bending, let yourself extend.[64]
These are the tubs in which you may truly float through
        the world;[65]
These are the three caves in which you may take cover.

117.

An omen of the winds of decline exists in the center of
        plentitude.
The mechanisms of germination exist in the midst of
        ruin.
Therefore, the gentleman knows,
    When living at ease, he must secure his right mind
    And contemplate affliction;
    In times of calamity, he must harden his fortitude one
        hundredfold
    And chart the route to success.

118.

Those who admire the unusual or take delight in the
uncommon
Do not have far-reaching discrimination.
Those who hold to a rigid integrity[66] or stiff self-reliance
Do not have long-lasting honor.

119.

When the flames of anger or the floods of desire
are about to boil over,
Consider these things with clarity,
And with clarity strike them down.
Who is it that knows?
Who is it that strikes?
If you are able to take this point
and turn it resolutely in your mind,
The twisted demon will become the gentleman of truth.

120.

Do not believe in the one-sided
nor be cheated by deceivers.
Do not be too self-reliant
nor make a show of your courage.

Do not, with your own strong points, expose the
shortcomings of others.
Do not, because of your own ineptitude,
despise abilities not your own.

121.

People's shortcomings—you need to patch them up with
grace.
If you drag them into the light of day and hoist them
up to view,
You will be attacking another's shortcomings with
your own.
People's intransigence—you need to enlighten them with
skill.
If you become angry and detest this chore,
You will be polishing another's intransigence with
your own.

122.

When encountering a gentleman of deep reticence,
Do not for a moment communicate your true mind.
When meeting a man of high-strung self-satisfaction,
Do your best to keep him from opening his mouth.

123.

When your thoughts are dismal and scattered,
    You should remember both awareness and caution.
When your thoughts are pressing and tense,
    You should remember looseness and composure.
Lacking this, though you may be able to get over the
        disease of depression,[67]
Won't the confusion of indecision inflict itself again?

124.

Even cloudless days and clear weather
May quickly change to sudden thunderclaps
        and shuddering streaks of lightning.
Even violent squalls and angry rains
May quickly change to a bright moon
        and a cloudless sky.
    What consistency has nature's movements?
    A stagnation as slender as an autumn hair.
    What consistency has the Cosmic Beginning?
    A hindrance as slender as a hair in the fall.
The carriage of man's mind should also be like this.

125.

Of the means for defeating the ego and suppressing desire,
It is said that if your understanding is slow,
your strength will not be easily applied.
And even if your understanding can penetrate the matter,
you may be unable to follow it through to the end.
Perhaps knowledge is the grain of the bright gem that
shines down on demons,
And strength is one flourish of the keen sword
that cuts them down.
We cannot lessen either.

126.

Though you are aware of the deceit of others,
Do not let this appear in words.
Though you receive the contempt of others,
Do not let this move your temper.
Between the two of these there is an infinity of meaning.
Between the two of these there is an infinity of use.

127.

Misfortune and distress—
This is a set of forges for tempering the great man.
  If one is able to bear this tempering, both body and mind benefit.
  If one is unable to bear it,
    both body and mind suffer loss.

128.

My body is a tiny Heaven and Earth.
  If joy and anger are not misguided,
  If likes and aversions are regulated,
    it will all be a harmonious scheme.
Heaven and Earth are our great parents.
  If people do not become hateful or succumb to grief,
  If all things in creation are neither hindered nor harmed, all phenomena will be at peace.

129.

"We should not seek to harm others
Nor should we *not* protect ourselves."
  This is a warning about being careless with our thoughts.

"It is better to be deceived by men
Than to be always looking for their lies."

This is a reprimand against betraying our insights.
When the two exist side by side,
There will be both clarity and concord.

130.

Do not inhibit your own beliefs because of public doubt.
Do not entrust yourself to your own ideas, and discard the words of others.
Do not add small benefits to yourself while utterly wearing yourself down.
Do not appropriate public opinion to accommodate your own emotions.

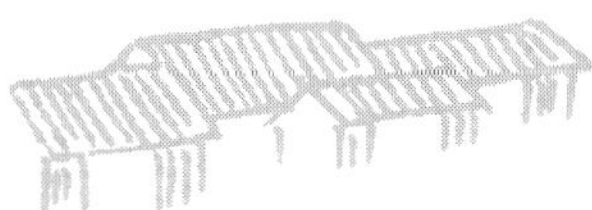

131.

While not yet on intimate terms with a good man,
It is best not to praise him in advance or you may call down on yourself the slander of scoundrels.
While not yet able to get away from a bad man,
It is best not to condemn him too quickly or you may invite a disaster that will ferment like yeast.

132.

Honor as clear as the day or as bright as the sun
    Is cultivated in dark rooms and deep recesses.[68]
Statecraft that could turn the universe on its course
    Is conducted as you might approach deep pools or
        tread on thin ice.

133.

A father acts with affection, a child with filial piety.
An elder brother acts with friendship, a younger brother
        with respect.
    Even if such behavior is carried to the utmost,
    Altogether, it is only as it should be,
And should not impress us by even a hairbreadth.
When a person who acts assumes virtue
And the person who receives feels obligation,
    It is the same as meeting a stranger on the road,
    Or bartering for goods in the market.

134.

If radiant beauty exists,
the ugly will necessarily exist to oppose it.[69]
But if I do not take pride in beauty,
Who will be able to consider me ugly?
If immaculate purity exists, the filthy will necessarily exist
to counter it.
But if I am not fond of purity,
Who will be able to contaminate me?

135.

Emotions arising like flames or chill winds—
These are much more intense among the wealthy and
ranked than among the poor and humble.
Minds full of jealousy and spite—
These are much more pronounced among relatives
than among strangers.
If you do not consider these points coolly
Or manage yourself with tranquility
Your ability to restrain deluding passions and desires
Will day by day decrease.

136.

Merit and misjudgment should not be confused;
If confusion exists, people's hearts will be invested with
negligence and sloth.
Gratitude and thanklessness should not be made too clear;
If clarity exists, people's thoughts will be sown with
division and doubt.[70]

137.

Title and rank should not be elevated too high.
Once a high elevation is reached, there is danger.
Ability should not be used to exhaustion.
Once exhaustion is reached, there is decline.
Moral behavior should not be raised excessively.
Once excess is reached, there will only come slander
and blame.

138.

Evil abhors the dark;
Good shies away from the light.[71]
Therefore:
When evil is manifest, its harm is superficial;

Hidden, its harm is profound.
When good is manifest, its merit is insignificant;
Hidden, its merit is great.

139.

Character is the master of talent, talent the servant of character.
To have talent but no character
Is like a house with the master absent and the servant in control.
How many times will the little demons[72] appear?
How many times run amok?

140.

In weeding out scoundrels or cutting off flatterers,
It is necessary to leave them a means of escape.
If you deal with them but leave no way out,
It is stopping up the hole of a mouse:
When all means of escape have been totally blocked,
It will chew its way through everything you love best.

141.

Accept blame along with others,
But do not accept praise.
When praise is shared, there will be mutual dislike.
Take a share in the suffering of others,
But do not take a share in their ease.
When ease is shared, there will be mutual dislike.

142.

If a gentleman of rank is impoverished and unable to help others,[73]
When meeting those deluded by their own foolishness
He will proffer words to awaken them.
When meeting others who are in imminent danger,
He will proffer words to save them.
This, too, is measureless charity.

143.

When hungry, they cling to you like vines;
  When full, they fly away like the wind.
If there is warmth, they trot right over;
  Where there is cold, they abandon ship.
These are the common evils of human nature.
The gentleman should cleanse and purify his composed vision.
But, with respect, not stand thoughtlessly obstinate in his views.

144.

One's character improves according to his magnanimity;
His magnanimity increases according to his consciousness.
Therefore, he who wishes to enrich his character
  Cannot do so without broadening his magnanimity.
He who wishes to broaden his magnanimity
  Cannot do so without increasing his consciousness.

145.

When the single lamp in my room flickers like a firefly,
And the music of all creation is suspended,
    I enter a peaceful solitude.
When first waking from the dreams of dawn,
And the bustling of the crowds has not yet begun,
    I leave the chaos of pre-creation.
Riding these moments, if I concentrate and reflect,
Letting wisdom shine and glow,[74]
I know first that
    My eyes, ears, mouth, and nose are all shackles;
    My emotions, desires, tastes, and predilections are but
        tricks and schemes.

146.

For the person open to self-examination,
Everything he touches turns to curing and medicinal
        goods.
For the person who blames others,
There are spears and halberds when his heart is stirred.
    The one opens up the road to all that is good;
    The other opens the springboard for all that is evil.
They are as different as Heaven and Earth.

147.

Although your deeds and writings follow the body
        and crumble into nothingness,
    The spirit is made anew for ten thousand ages.
Although merit and name, wealth and rank follow the
        world in its mutability,
    For honor and high-mindedness, one thousand years is
        the same as one day.
The gentleman truly should not change one for the other.

148.

The net is set for the fish,
    But catches the swan in its mesh.[75]
The praying mantis covets its prey,
    While the sparrow approaches from the rear.
Within one contrivance hides another;
Beyond one change, another is born.
Are wisdom and skill enough to put your hopes on?

149.

Being human, if you possess not even a sliver of sincerity
in your heart,
You will become nothing more than a beggar,
And all your affairs will be shams;
Passing through this world,
If you possess neither a grain of gentleness nor an
affable disposition,
You will be nothing more than a wooden dummy:
Everywhere you go you will find obstructions.

150.

If no waves arise, water will settle of itself;
If no shadows cross it, the mirror will naturally be bright.
Thus, the heart cannot be *made* pure, but if you avoid
muddying elements
Purity will appear on its own.
Thus, pleasure should not be sought after, but if you
avoid things that cause suffering,
Pleasure will exist on its own.

151.

With just one thought,
You can offend the commandments of the divine spirits.[76]
With just one word,
You can injure the harmony of Heaven and Earth.
With just one action,
You can bring disaster on your descendents.
You should take extreme caution.

152.

Among things, there are those not well understood when hurried,
But when approached leisurely, become clear of their own accord:
Do not be impatient, and thus hasten others' wrath.
In putting men to use, there are those who will not follow,
But when left on their own, change by themselves:
Be lenient in controlling others, so as not to increase their obstinacy.

153.

Having pride in your own integrity, looking down on
        high rank and office;
Creating compositions more refined than famous works:
    If you do not knead your moral character like fine
        porcelain clay,
    In the end it is just like egotistical false courage:
    Clever but of poor workmanship.

154.

When resigning from an office,[77]
    You should resign at the height of your strength.
When finding a place for yourself,
    You should look for a place where you can be alone.
When being purposeful about your conduct,
    You should be so in the smallest detail.
When conferring favors,
    You should confer them on those
        unable to pay you back.

155.

Rather than associating with city people,
Make friends with the old folks who live in the mountains.
Rather than having audiences in crimson palaces,
Become intimate with those who live in thatched huts.
Rather than listening in on the talks of streets and ports,
Let your ears be filled with the songs of woodcutters and cowherds.
Rather than talking about your contemporaries' vices and blunders,
Relate the fine sayings and actions of the men of old.

156.

Character is the foundation of achievement.
Where the foundation is not secure,
There is yet to be a structure firm and long-lasting.
The heart is the root of one's descendents.
Where the root is not well planted,
There are yet to be flourishing branches and leaves.

157.

A man of former times spoke against,[78]

"Throwing away your own inexhaustible storehouse,
And imitating the indigents who hold their bowls and line the gates."

Another has said,[79]

"Nouveau riche with indigent souls! Take a break from preaching dreams!
Will fire from the stove of any house not make the smoke rise?"

One verse warns against being blind to your own possessions.
The other remonstrates against pride in what you own.
Both can be important precepts for the student.

158.

The Way is in the public domain,
And all should be encouraged to seek it.
Learning is a like a daily meal,
And its nourishment should be strongly recommended to all.

159.

About the man who believes in others
    While others may not be entirely sincere:
    Sincerity will reside in him alone.
About the man who doubts others
    While others may not be wholly fraudulent:
    Fraud will reside in him from the first.

160.

When your heart is all-embracing and kind,
It is like the spring breeze that warms and nurtures:
    All that meet you will grow.
When your heart is cold and severe,
It is like the northern snow that pales and stiffens all things:
    All that meet you will wither.

161.

Doing good without seeking profit
    Is like the melon growing among weeds:
    It develops unseen of its own accord.
Committing evil without aiming to harm
    Is like the spring snow lying in the garden:
    It should melt naturally away, without note.

162.

When meeting old acquaintances,
    Your feelings should be animated all the more.
When doing something hidden from view,[80]
    Your frame of mind should be all the more on display.
When waiting on others well past their prime,
    Your cordiality should be ever amplified.

163.

The word *exertion* originally counseled people to a moral
        sense,
    But the public has borrowed the term
    To deliver them from poverty.
The word *thrift* originally lightened the people's sense of
        wealth,
    But the public has temporarily usurped the term
    To embellish stinginess.
What the gentleman uses as a charm for his preservation,
The small-minded employ to build their selfishness.
    Regrettable, indeed!

164.

Practicing certain conduct only when the interest arises,
You will sometimes practice, but sometimes cease to do so.
How can you consider this progress without backsliding?[81]
Being enlightened only as your emotions dictate,
You will sometimes be enlightened, but sometimes be in doubt.
In the end, this will not be the lamp of eternal light.[82]

165.

Tolerate the mistakes and faults of others,
But not your own.
Endure your own difficulties and disgrace,
But not those of others.

166.

To rid yourself of worldliness is extraordinary.
Yet to deliberately respect the ordinary
Will not make you so: it will only make you look strange.
To remain aloof from the world's contamination is purity.
Yet to sever ties with the world and seek the pure
Will not make you so: it will only make you look extreme.

167.

Favors conferred should at first be slight, and then more generous.
If they are generous at first and later slight,
People will forget their benefit.
Authority imposed should at first be strict, and then more lenient.
If it is lenient at first and later strict,
People will resent its severity.

168.

If the mind is empty,
your true nature[83] becomes manifest.
If you do not shut off the mind,

It will be like stirring up the waves,
    Then looking for the reflection of the moon.
If the heart is unstained, the mind will be pure.
If you do not make your mind clear,
    It will be like seeking out a mirror,
    Your very action covering it in dust.

169.

When I have rank and people respect it,
    They are respecting my tall cap and great sash.
When I am destitute and people despise me,
    They are despising my cotton garb and straw sandals.
If this is so, they do not respect me from the first,
    So why should I be happy?
They do not despise me from the first,
    So why become upset?

170.

"For the sake of the mice, they always left out rice;
    In pity for the moths, they did not light the lamps."[84]
Thoughts like these of the people of old
Are the agencies that help us to flourish as human beings.
    Without them we are merely bodies
    Of earth and wood.

171.

The substance of the mind is nothing other than the
substance of the universe.
Thoughts of joy: auspicious stars and promising clouds.
Thoughts of anger: rattling thunder and violent gales.
Thoughts of benevolence: soft winds and sweet dew.[85]
Thoughts of severity: hot summer days and autumn
frosts.
Which of these natural phenomena could you diminish?
It is necessary only to follow their rise and their
decrease,
To be fully open and to put up no barriers.
In this way you become one fabric with the origin of the
stars.

172.

In uneventful times,
The mind is easily distracted.
Then you should make yourself still and let your true
nature shine.
When things are happening all around you,
The mind is easily scattered,
Then you should make your true nature shine and allow
your center to become still.

173.

When you want to discuss a subject,
Put yourself outside the matter
And fathom the situation's advantages and disadvantages.
When you want to take up a matter,
Put yourself in the middle of the thing
And forget all reflections on profit and loss.

174.

When the true gentleman finds himself in a place of authority or importance,
He must conduct himself strictly in the light of day,
Keeping his mind both gentle and easy.
He must not let down his guard
And fall in with those who smell of self-interest or greed.
Nor must he follow extremes
And end up stung with the poison of his own scorpions and wasps.

175.

The man who makes honor his main attraction
  Is bound to receive ridicule.
The man who makes philosophy his signboard
  Forever invites fault-finding.
Therefore, the gentleman
  Neither approaches evil
  Nor seeks a reputation for being good.
  Only in the gem of harmonious concord does he
    reside.

176.

If you meet a deceiver,
  Move him with sincerity;
Of you meet a bully,
  Imbue him with harmony.
If you meet a perverse or self-seeking person,
  Encourage him with moral duty and integrity.
There is nothing under Heaven I cannot knead or mold.

177.

With even a touch of charity,
  You can brew harmony to fill Heaven and Earth.

With one small pinch of purity,
    You can bequeath a clarity and fragrance to last a hundred generations.

178.

Obscure plots and strange conventions,
Eccentric behavior and mysterious abilities—
    Together, these are the roots of disaster that spread throughout the world.
Only with ordinary virtues and ordinary behavior[86]
    Can you make your original nature replete
    And beckon harmony in.

179.

An old saying goes,
    "When climbing a mountain, you endure the steep roads;
    When walking through snow, you endure the narrow bridges."
The one word *endure*
Has considerable significance.
Human nature is steep, and the road through this world vexing.
    If people do not acquire endurance for support,
    Won't many fall into a thicket or ditch?

180.

Those who are proud of their accomplishments, or put up
their knowledge like lamps for all to see
Are relying on externals to make themselves men.
They should know that
When the mind shines like a jewel and one's original
nature is not lost,
Though they have performed no great deeds, nor have
knowledge of writing,
They will be naturally dignified and correct.
They become men of their own accord.

181.

When you are busy but want to steal leisure time,
Before enjoying it
Search out the right place for your mind.[87]
When the situation is chaotic and you want to find peace,
First, you must establish the mind's autonomy earlier,
When you *are* at peace.
If this is not done,
You will be tossed about by your surroundings,
Or flutter like a flag in the wind of events.

182.

Do not let your mind become clouded,
Do not deplete the good will of others,
Do not exhaust the vigor of things.
With these three,
    You will be able to establish your mind in accord with Heaven and Earth,
    Bring your fate into balance with that of the people,
    And build a good estate for the sake of your descendents.

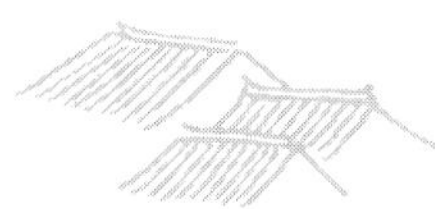

183.

When working in an official capacity,
Follow two modes of advice.
As they say,
    If there is impartiality, clarity will grow.
    If there is honesty, authority will grow.
When at home,
There are two kinds of advice.
As they say,
    If there is sympathy,[88] emotions will be at peace.
    If there is thrift, what is used will be sufficient.

184.

When in a place of wealth and rank,
Pay attention to the suffering of the poor and humble.
During the time of your youth and vigor,
Guide your thoughts to the hardships of the old and feeble.[89]

185.

In carrying yourself through the world,
Do not try to be overly pure.
One needs to ingest
A morsel of disgrace and defacement, too.
In associating with others,
Do not be too scrupulous.
One needs to embrace
Both the good and the evil, both the clever and the dull.

186.

Give up confronting little men;
Little men will, of themselves, confront each other.
Give up fawning upon men of high quality;
Men of high quality are, from the beginning, without self-interest.

187.

The disease of blatant desire can be cured,
But the disease of excuse-making is difficult to alleviate.
The obstacles of external affairs and things can be
displaced,
But the obstacles of Reason are difficult to remove.

188.

Polishing and burnishing yourself
Is comparable to forging metal a hundred times:
The man who prepares himself too quickly will have no
deep breeding at all.
Undertaking a task with competence
Is comparable to pulling a stone bow of a thousand
pounds:
The man who shoots lightly will have no effect at all.

189.

It is better to incur the displeasure of small men
Than to receive their flattery.
It is better to receive the criticism of men of high quality
Than to obtain their toleration.

190.

Those who love profit run along the outside of the Way:
    Their mischief is apparent and shallow.
Those who love fame hide like mice in
        the burrow of the Way:
    Their mischief is hidden and deep.

191.

Receiving a favor, and though it is considerable,
    Not repaying it;
Drawing enmity, and though it is light,
    Returning it in style;
Hearing of ill deeds, and though they are unclear,
    Having no doubt about them;
Then, when good is apparent, doubting it altogether—
    Such ways are the far end of cruelty;
    This is brutality in the extreme.
You should be careful about this.

192.

Slanderers and gossips
Are like thin clouds covering the sun:

It will not be long before they clear up of themselves.
Flatterers and toadies
Resemble the gusts of wind that brush our flesh:
One is not conscious of any damage.

193.

On high mountain peaks, there are no trees,
but in river valleys and meandering places
Grasses and trees grow dense.
Where water swirls or moves rapidly, there are no fish,
but in deep pools and quiet places
Fishes and turtles congregate.
Thus is the gentleman extremely cautious
Of lofty actions
Or quick emotions.

194.

Of those who have accomplished great deeds
or established important enterprises,
Many were unprejudiced and harmonious fellows.
But those who have muddled affairs
or lost their chances,
Were invariably men of attachment and obstinacy.

195.

Living in the world,
You should not imitate what is common,
  But should not deviate from it either.
Conducting events,
You should not make people angry,
    nor should you make them glad.

196.

When the sun is setting,
Patterns of haze and mist become all the more brilliant.
When the year comes to its end,
The oranges and tangerines are all the more fragrant.[90]
Thus, on the road to his later years,
  The gentleman should quicken his spirit
    one hundredfold.

197.

When the hawk soars, it looks asleep.
When the tiger walks, it seems to be ailing.
But in truth, this is their means of seizing their prey.
Thus the gentleman
  Should not let his wisdom show,
  Nor give his ability free play.

Only then will he have the capacity
To shoulder the vast and carry the weighty.

198.

Thrift is a beautiful virtue.
But if it goes too far, it becomes stinginess
  Or a vulgar miserliness,
And damages the True Way.
Deference to others is excellent behavior.
But if it goes too far, it becomes excessive politeness[91]
  Or a twisted reverence,
And may give birth to twisted designs.

199.

Do not be distressed when events turn counter to your
    wishes;
Do not be overjoyed when things go your way.
Do not count on lengthy contentment;
Do not shy away from first difficulties.

200.

Those who take pleasure in banquets and drinking bouts
Do not have good households.
Those who struggle for reputation and showiness
Are not true gentlemen.
Those who think too much about name and position
Are not good administrators.

201.

People think pleasure satisfies the mind,
But in seeking pleasure
They are drawn into suffering.
The accomplished think pleasure runs against their hearts' desire;
And in the end, it is through suffering
That pleasure is gained.

202.

A life of total satisfaction is like water
Rising to the lip of the jug,
But not overflowing:
Even one more drop would be too much.

A life in a state of crisis is like a tree
Sawn nearly through
But not quite toppling:
Even one slight push would bring it down.

203.

A cool eye discerns men's character.
A cool ear hears the intent of their speech.
Cool emotions plumb others' feelings.
A cool mind thinks through Principle.[92]

204.

The mind of a man of humanity is loose and at ease;[93]
With his fortune ample and his happiness extended,
His spirit is carefree in every situation.
The thoughts of a mean-hearted man are cramped and constrained;
With his happiness shallow and his prosperity short,
He looks restless at every turn.

205.

Hearing of evil, do not be quick to rile:
    It may be a slanderer giving vent to his ire.
Hearing of good works, do not hastily advance
        friendship:
    It may be the wicked enticing you.

206.

The man whose mind is quick-tempered and rude
Accomplishes not one thing.
For the man whose mind is harmonious and calm,
One hundred blessings gather of themselves.

207.

In employing others,
    Do not be too strict.
    Otherwise, those who exert themselves will leave.
In making friends,
    Do not go to extremes.
    Otherwise, flatterers will soon be at your side.

208.

When the wind is blustery and the rain falls
Suddenly, you should stand and plant your feet.
When the flowers are in full bloom and the willows most charming,
You should fix your sights a little higher.
When the road is dangerous and the narrow paths steep,
You should do an about-face without delay.

209.

The man of high integrity
Redeems himself with a sense of harmony,
And only then keeps the road to quarrel unopened.
The man of distinguished service
Complies with a sense of humility,
And from the first keeps the gates of jealousy closed.

210.

The high official—
In office, he should exercise moderation in his writings
and letters
So as to make it difficult for others to see through him,
Thus obstructing opportunistic schemes.
When retired to the country, he should not appear so
elevated as cliffs and peaks
but make it easy for others to see him,
Thus making old friendships more cordial.

211.

You should stand in awe of great men.[94]
Doing so,
Your mind will contain no self-indulgence.
You should stand in awe of the humble.
Doing so,
You will have no reputation as high-handed.

212.

When events run a little against your desires,
Direct your thoughts to those who are not as well off.
Then resentment and blame[95] will of themselves
disappear.
When your mind becomes a bit slovenly,
Direct your thoughts to those who have excelled beyond
your own lot.
Then your spirits will of themselves be restored.

213.

Do not be carried away with happiness
and lightly give your consent.
Do not be carried away by drunkenness
and give rise to your anger.
Do not be carried away with lighthearted compliance
and make your affairs many.
Do not be carried away by disinterest
and lessen your final efforts.

214.

The person who reads books carefully
Should read until "his hands dance and his feet stamp";[96]
Then, from the first, he will not fall into "net and snares."[97]
The person who perceives things well
Should look until his mind merges and his spirit softens;
Then, from the first, the outward traces will not be muddied.

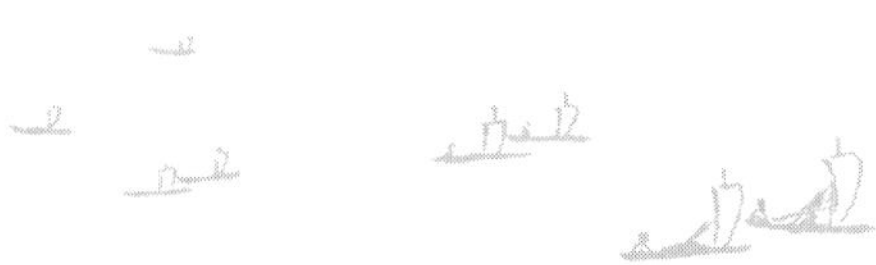

215.

Heaven makes a man wise to enlighten the ignorance of the people.
But in the world, he acts contrarily and strengthens his own talents,
Thus exposing the shortcomings of others.
Heaven makes a man wealthy to relieve the difficulties of the people.
But in the world, he acts contrarily, and bear-hugs his own possessions,[98]
Thus ignoring the poverty of others.
Truly men to be cut down by Heaven.[99]

216.

The man who has arrived[100] has neither anxiety nor
apprehension;[101]
The ignorant man has no discrimination, no knowledge.
Together they can talk about Learning;
Together they can work through their projects.
The man who is half-wise is full
Of anxieties, apprehensions, judgments, and the usual
bits of knowledge;
His aspirations are many and ordinary.
If you work with him, nothing will come easy.

217.

The mouth is surely the mind's gate.
When the mouth is not guarded closely,
All of your secrets will spill over and out.
Thoughts are surely the mind's feet.
When thoughts are not strictly protected,
Heresies and shortcuts will rush right in.

218.

If the person who criticizes others
Will root out successes in the midst of faults,
No one will be chagrined.
If the person who examines himself
Will look for faults in the midst of his successes,
His character will gain ground.

219.

The young man is the embryo of the adult;
The clever student, of the high official.
At this stage,
If the strength of the fire is insufficient,
The casting will not be pure.
On a later day,
When he goes through the world, or stands at court,
It will be difficult to be of good use.

220.

When the gentleman suffers difficulties, he is not distressed;
But finding himself at the banquet table,
He shrinks back in fear and unease.

When meeting a man of influence and power, he does not
miss a beat;
But encountering the distressed and lonely,
His mind is unsettled and tense.

221.

Though plum and damson are charming,
How can they compare with the steadfast green
of pine and oak?
Though pear and apricot are sweet,
How can they measure up to the sharp fragrance
of bitter orange and green tangerine?[102]
In truth, the colorful and short-lived
Are not equal to the light-hued and longstanding;
And easy beauty
Does not measure up to slow but steady growth.

222.

In the midst of a tranquil breeze and quiet waves,
You see the true form of human life.
Where exist the simple-tasting and tranquil-voiced,
You detect the original nature of the mind.

BOOK TWO

1.

The man who talks about the pleasures of mountain and
forest[1]
May not divine the true content of such places.
He who shudders at conversations about fame and profit
May not yet have forgotten such themes.

2.

A fishing line in the water is an aesthetic thing,
But now you hold the rod of life or death.
The game of *go* is a tasteful sport,
But it also incites the mind to conflict.
Clearly:
Taking pleasure in something is not equal
To the suitability of lessening one's affairs;
Having many abilities does not measure up
To the fulfillment of having none at all.

3.

The profusion of songbirds and blossoms,
The depth of the mountains,
The charm of the valley—
These are surely the illusory conditions of Heaven and
Earth.

The dried-up streams, falling trees,[2]
The wearing away of stones,
The crumbling of cliffs—
Here alone can you see the true Self of the world.

4.

Time is, by its nature, long;
But the preoccupied man hurries restlessly along.
Heaven and Earth are, by their nature, expansive;
But the mean of heart are naturally narrow.
The seasons' breezes, flowers, snow, and moon are, by their nature, tranquil;
But the man who toils and fusses is afflicted of his own free will.

5.

Obtaining the tasteful does not come from owning many things;
Between a tray-sized pond and a fist-sized stone
You have sufficient implements for mists and hazy scenes.
Landscapes that will meet your desires are not far away:
Through a mugwort-lined window or beneath a bamboo hut,
Wind and moon are of themselves calm.

6.

Listening to the sound of a bell during a peaceful night,
I am called into sobriety from my dream within a dream.[3]
Watching the reflection of the moon in the clear deep pool,
I catch a glimpse of the body beyond this earthly shell.

7.

The chirping of birds, the cries of insects—
All are secret communications of the mind.
The brilliance of flowers, the colors of grasses—
These are nothing other than literary patterns of the manifest Way.

The man who studies such things
Must purify his natural capabilities,
Give his heart the timbre of the sound of jewels,
And come to grasp this truth in everything he touches.

8.

Men understand how to read books that have words,
But do not understand how to read those that lack them.
They know how to pluck the lute that has strings,
But do not know how to play the one that has none.[4]
Caught by the form, but untouched by the spirit:
How will they get at the heart of either music or literature?

9.

If the heart contains no worldly desires,
You will have autumnal skies and cloudless seas.
If you can sit with just a lute and a book,[5]
Wherever you are becomes the realm of the sages.[6]

10.

When guests and friends have gathered like clouds,
There is pleasure in furious and profuse cups of wine.
But suddenly the water clock leaks out its last,
the lanterns gutter,
the incense fades away,
the tea is cold;
Involuntarily there is weeping instead of joy,
And friends are left with a desolate, insipid taste.
This is generally the way things are in this world.
Why, then, don't we quickly change our minds?

11.

When you have grasped the core of a single thing,
The mists and moon of the Five Lakes[7]
Will be within your heart.
When you have broken through the secrets lying right
before your eyes,
One thousand heroes of old
Will be delivered to your grasp.

12.

Mountains and rivers and the great Earth
    Are already nothing but dust,[8]
While man, to be sure, is but dust within dust.
Bodies composed of muscle and blood
    Will surely return to bubble and shadow[9]
While human affairs, to be sure, are but shadows within
        shades.
    If the highest wisdom is not obtained,
    There will be no heart of understanding.

13.

Within the light of the flint's spark,
    They fight over "long" and compete over "short,"
    Yet how much time can there be?
Above the horns of the tiny snail,[10]
    They compare their losses and argue about gains,
    Yet how big can the world be?

14.

The cold lamp offers no flame,
The worn-out fur no warmth—
    Such things are only fooling with appearance.
A body resembling withered branches,
A heart like dead ashes[11]—
    This is only the degeneration of the obstinate ascetic.

15.

If you have the conviction to cease an action right now,
You will right now bring the matter to a close.
But if you need to look around for the moment to stop,
    Though the bride and groom may be all prepared,
    The petty details will go on and on.[12]
Though you may happily be ready to follow the Buddha
        or the Tao,
Your heart will still lack understanding.
The ancients said,
    If you quit right now, you will quit.
    If you look for the perfect time, it will not appear.
This is truly clear-sighted.

16.

When your passion is observed from a position of
serenity,
You know the zero profit of all that running around.
When entering a state of tranquility from an abundance
of cares,
You are aware that the savoring of peace outdistances
the rest.

17.

You may have the inclination to consider wealth and
position as insubstantial as floating clouds.[13]
And yet not have to seclude yourself among crags and
caves.
You may not be afflicted with an addiction
for nature's springs and rocks,
But still get tipsy on your own, and absorb yourself in
poems.

18.

Leave the fighting over name and wealth to others,
But do not despise their intoxication with such things.
Your own disinterestedness is appropriate for you,
But do not take pride in thinking that you alone are
        enlightened.[14]
This is what Shakamuni spoke of:
    Do not be wrapped up in doctrine;
    Do not be wrapped up in the Void.
    Body and mind are two, but totally free.

19.

The extended and contracted depend on the thought;
The broad and the narrow are affected by your mind.
Therefore, the composed man
    Considers one day longer than a thousand years.
The spacious of mind
    Sees a tiny room as expansive as Heaven and Earth.

20.

Decrease this[15] and decrease it again,
Plant flowers and set bamboo,
  And you will return all to the Void.
Forget that there is nothing to forget,
Burn incense and heat up some tea,
  And you'll not be troubled though no one comes
    bearing gifts of wine.[16]

21.

All the things right before your eyes—
  For the man who knows they are sufficient,
    this is the world of the sages.
  For the man who thinks them not enough,
    this is a world profane.
All the causes from which things issue into the world—
  For the man who puts them to use,
    they give life to all things.
  For the man who uses them poorly,
    they are the functions of death.

22.

The disasters that accompany
    Those who blaze like fire,[17]
    And those attached to the influential,
Are extraordinarily harsh and astonishingly swift.
The experience of those
    Who find harbor in composure,
    And who protect their own leisure,
Is astoundingly light and extremely long-lived.

23.

In a river valley of pines, I walk alone with staff in hand;
    Standing still for a moment,
    Clouds rise around my tattered robes.
Beneath a window looking out on bamboo, I stretch out with a book for my pillow.
    When I awake,
    The moon shines in on the cold, cracked floor.

24.

Physical desire may rage like fire,
But if you think of what happens when you get ill,
  Your fervor will turn cold as ashes.
Fame and fortune may be as sweet as candy,
But if you consider the place of your death,
  They will seem like chewing wax.
Therefore,
  If a man will always take to time think of death,
    and ruminate on illness
  The works of illusion will disappear,
    and the Way-seeking mind will endure.

25.

The alleys and bypaths of fighting to get ahead are
    narrow.
  But step back a pace, and that pace will be broad and
    wide.
The taste of the voluptuous and rich is short.
  But make yourself just one percent plain and pure, and
    that one percent will become calm and composed.

26.

If you wish to avoid falling into confusion
when busily occupied,
Cultivate your mind and make it pure during your leisure
hours.
If you wish to avoid extreme agitation
at the moment of death,
Observe the world and see through it while still alive.

27.

In the forest of seclusion, there is no honor or disgrace;
On the road of right conduct, no flaming up or cooling
down.

28.

You need not seek protection from the heat of the day;
But if you seek protection from the distress of thinking of the heat,
Your body will always sit on a platform both refreshing and cool.
You may not be able to drive away a devastating poverty;
But if you drive away the unhappiness of being in such a state,
Your mind will always reside in a house of pleasure and peace.

29.

When about to advance a step,
Quickly think about retreating one step, too:
Thus you can avoid the disaster of getting stuck in the hedge.[18]
When about to grasp at something,
Consider first letting it go:
Thus you can escape the danger of riding the tiger's back.[19]

30.

About the man who is greedy:

Though money is parceled out, he will resent not receiving jewels.

Though commissioned with public office, he will grumble about not acquiring a fief.

Though influential and powerful, he will still happily behave in a beggarly way.

About the man who knows sufficiency:

He considers his plain herb soup tastier than fatty meats or high-class rice.

He considers his padded coat warmer than a robe of fox or badger skins.[20]

Though one of the commoners, he is not less satisfied than a nobleman.

31.

Being proud of your name

Does not compare with fleeing fame altogether.

Becoming skillful at something

Is not like avoiding externals and having time on your own.

32.

The man who has a taste for quietism
Looks into the white clouds and hazy crags,
        and becomes intimate with the mysterious.[21]
The man who runs after the magnificent
Watches sublime dances and beautiful chants,
        and forgets all fatigue.
    Only for the man who is satisfied with himself
    Is there neither tumult or quiet,
    Neither the magnificent nor the withered.
There is no place he can go that is not appropriate for him.

33.

A single cloud leaves the peaks:[22]
    Going or staying, with neither is it entangled.
A bright mirrorlike moon hangs in the sky:
    Peace or noise, with neither is it concerned.

34.

A tendency for deliberation and composure
Is not obtained while drinking strong wines,
But rather while sipping simple bean soup and drinking plain water.[23]
A sense of pathos and compassion
Is not developed from the dry and solitary,
But rather from blowing the bamboo flute and plucking the lute.
This is known to be true:
The taste of the thick and rich is always short,
While the meaning of the simple and plain alone is truth.

35.

In Zen it is said:
When hungry, eat your rice;
When fatigued, sleep.[24]
In the deep meaning of poetry it is said,
The scenery is right before your eyes;
The words are always on your tongue.
Ultimately, the highest principle resides in the plainest notion;
The most difficult emerges from the very easy.

That which is "full of meaning" is, on the contrary, far away;
While "No-Mind" is, in truth, nearby.

36.

The water flows, but no sound is there:
From this we grasp the meaning of seeing peace
in the midst of tumult.
The mountains are high, but the clouds are unobstructed:
From this we awake to the chance of passing from
existence to nonexistence.

37.

Mountains and forests—excellent places.
But once you place designs on them,
They become no better than the marketplace.
Books and paintings—elegant things.
But once they are coveted unreasonably,
They are no better than pawned goods.
Generally, if the mind is untainted,
Even the vulgar world is the realm of the sages.
But if the mind is infatuated,
Even places of pleasure become seas of regret.

38.

The moment there is noise and confusion,
    Even the things we remember from day to day
    Are all forgotten, one after another.
In a moment of clarity and peace,
    Even the things we have forgotten long ago
    Appear before our very eyes.
Thus we perceive:
    If peace and boisterousness are separated but a little,
    Darkness and light will be suddenly distinct.

39.

Under a comforter of reeds, I lie down in the snow,
        sleeping above the clouds.
And, in a single room, I am able to preserve
The refreshing force of the night's serenity.
Well into my cups, I chant into the wind,
        playing under the moon.
Thus can I take this body and hide it away,
Ten thousand leagues from
        the world's crimson dust.

40.

If, in the procession of a high official,
There is one mountain recluse with a goosefoot staff,
It increases the train's lofty character by at least a degree.
If, on the road of fishermen and woodcutters,
There is one court official in ceremonial robes,
It adds vulgarity to the place by no small measure.
Know this well:
The rich is not superior to the plain;
The worldly does not stand up to the unsullied.

41.

The way of transcending the world
Exists in passing the world right through.
It is not necessary to cut people off,
and thus avoid the world.
The means of understanding your mind
Exists in using it completely.[25]
It is not necessary to cut off your desires,
and thus turn the mind to ashes.

42.

If this body could be forever released to a place of true
leisure,
Who would be able to drive me away
With honor or shame, gain or loss?
If this mind could forever exist in the midst of inactivity,
Who would be able to deceive or cheat me
With right or wrong, profit or harm?

43.

Walking along a bamboo hedge,
Unexpectedly I hear a dog bark, a cock crow,[26]
And somehow I'm in a world amidst the clouds.
Sitting in my book-lined room,
I hear the continuing cicada's cry, the crow's noisy caw,
And now I perceive the universe of peace.

44.

If I do not seek prosperity,
Why should I be troubled by the sweet-smelling bait
        of profit or reward?
If I do not compete to get ahead,
Why should I fear the certain danger
        of working for the state?

45.

Rambling among the mountains and forests, springs and
        rocks,
The mind soiled by the dust of the world gradually
        expires.
Playing leisurely with poetry and books, paintings and
        sketches,
The spirit of the vulgar quietly ceases.
Therefore, the gentleman
    Does not take pleasure in material things or lose his
        free will;[27]
    But makes use of another land and pacifies his mind.

46.

Spring days have an air of prosperity and bustle,
And we feel expansive and at ease.
But this cannot equal the days of autumn
When clouds are white and winds are pure,
Orchids fragrant and the cassia sweet-smelling,
The moonlight shines high in the heavens above,
and is reflected in the rivers and streams below,
Making us pure in body and mind.

47.

If you have not memorized a single Chinese character,
But possess the meaning of poetry,
You have obtained poetry's substance.
If you have not recited a single *gatha*,[28]
But possess the taste of Zen,
You are awake to the mysteries of its teachings.

48.

If your nerves are agitated,
You will look at the shadow of a bow and imagine
a snake or scorpion.
You will look at stationary rocks and suspect
tigers crouched in waiting.
In this frame of mind, everything contains a mortal danger.
If your thoughts have been suspended,
You can make violent men as gentle as sea gulls,
You can hear the frog's croak as the sound of drum and
flute.
In everything you touch, you will see the play of truth.

49.

The body is like an unmoored boat:[29]
Whether it proceeds or is thwarted
Is only up to the current.
The mind resembles a dried-up tree:
How can it be hindered
By cleaving swords or daubs of cosmetics?

50.

The human heart
  Listens to the nightingale sing and thereupon rejoices;
  Hears the frog croak and is thereupon annoyed;
  Observes the flowers bloom and immediately thinks of gardening;
  Comes upon some weeds and promptly reaches for the hoe.
This approach judges a thing by feeling its form.
Look carefully at an object through its true nature.
Then, no matter what it may be,
  What does not, of its own, sing of nature's play?
  What does not, by itself, look to its own growth?

51.

Hair thinning, teeth falling out—
  Leave that to the withering of the temporal form.
Birds singing, flowers blooming—
  Know this to be the true reality[30] of your own nature.[31]

52.

Filled with desire,
You are like waves seething over a cold abyss:
Even in mountains and forests, you will not see peace.
Filled with Emptiness,
You are like a cool breeze born from intense heat:
Even in town and market, you will not know noise.

53.

The person who hoards much may lose enormously.
Therefore know that wealth is not equal
To having no apprehensions of poverty.
The person who climbs high may quickly fall headfirst.
Therefore know that high status is not equal
To being at ease without it.

54.

Reading the *I Ching* by the window at dawn,
I grind red notation ink with dew from pine branches.
Discussing the sutras at my desk in the afternoon,
The sound of the clear gong is carried by the wind
beneath the bamboo.

55.

When flowers are put in a tray,
They lose the force of life.
When birds are put in a cage,
Their natural instincts quickly decline.
Better to
    Have flowers and birds in the mountains,
    Mix and flock together, producing their patterns,
    Flying about at their own free will,
    Spontaneously carefree and
        in harmony with themselves.

56.

Simply because people in this world
        rely too much on the truth of "self,"
    Preferences and desires are many and sundry,
    Many and sundry are passions and lusts.
A man of former times[32] said,
    If I did not know the self existed,
    How would I know the desirability of things?
Someone[33] also said,
    If you know that the body is not the self,
    How can lusts and passions be a bother?
These are truly penetrating words.

57.

Looking at youth from the vantage point of impending old age,
You can extinguish the mind
That goes chasing about, competing for fortune and fame.
Looking at prosperous years from the light of someday being sick and broken,
You will be able to cut off thoughts
Of the gay and gaudy life.

58.

Social conditions and the human heart
Quickly change from one thing to the next:
We should not look to either for the Great Truth.
Yao Fu[34] said,
In times long past, "myself" was said to be a certain person;
But now, on the contrary, I believe that person was someone else.
Thus, I don't know—the person I am today
I may consider to be someone else in the future.
If we could always use this view,
The vexations we hold within would quickly disappear.

59.

If in the midst of passion and din,
You keep your eye cool and unmoved,
You will eliminate many bitter thoughts.
If in a place of hard and unfavorable circumstances,
You keep your mind passionately enthused,
You will obtain an abundance of true grace.

60.

For every pleasant situation,
There is an unpleasant one waiting to be its complement.
For every desirable condition,
There is an undesirable one checking and balancing.
Just eating your daily meals
And enjoying your usual surrounding—
Only in this is the dwelling of peace and joy.

61.

From a latticed window looking out on a broad and lofty
view,
I see the blue mountains and green waters with
clouds and mists passing in and out
And am aware of the freedom of All That Is.
In the bamboo thickets and luxurious branches and leaves,
I observe nursing swallows and cooing doves[35]
greeting and sending off the seasons,
And know how to forget that the external and I are two.

62.

Knowing that achievement must inevitably fall apart,
The mind seeking achievement
Will not be too relentless or rigid.
If you know that what is born must inescapably die,
The Path that prolongs life
Will not necessarily be too demanding.

63.

Ku Te[36] said,

The shadow of the bamboo sweeps the steps,
but the dust is unmoved.
The ring of the moon glides across the pond,
but in the water there is no trace.

One of our Confucian scholars[37] said,

Though the waters flow rapidly,
the surroundings are always serene.
Though the flowers fall repeatedly,
the mind is of itself at peace.

If we could always maintain these thoughts
When we react to events and encounter external things,
How free our bodies and minds would be.

64.

The echo of the wind through the pines;
The voice of the spring flowing over the rocks:
When I come to listen while at peace within,
I understand they are the exquisite sounds of Heaven
and Earth, of the Of-Itself-So.
The haze that spreads at the edge of the field;
The shadow of the clouds in the waters' depths:
When I go to look within while at ease without,

I perceive them to be the highest patterns
of Heaven and Earth.

65.

With their eyes they see the hazels and brambles
beneath which lie the ruins of the Western Tsin;[38]
Yet still they are proud of their shining swords.
The bodies buried at Pe Mang[39] are now prey
for foxes and hares;
Yet still more they long for their yellow gold.
As the saying goes:
Wild animals are easy to subjugate,
But man's mind is overcome with difficulty;
A canyon is easy to fill in,
But man's mind is difficult to fulfill with toil.
Surely this is true.

66.

When over the ground of the mind,
there is no wind or waves,
Wherever you go,
will be blue mountains and green trees.
When within your innate character,
there is change and growth,
Wherever you are,
will be jumping fish and soaring hawks.

67.

An official who wears an imposing hat and wide sash
At some time,
Watching those wrapped in light straw coats and small umbrellas,
Passing their time pleasantly and lightheartedly,
Must surely sigh and feel envious.
The wealthy man who perches atop large mats and wide rugs
At some time,
Dealing with those who sit at coarse rattan blinds and plain desks,
Passing their time leisurely and at peace,
Must surely sour with yearning and regret.

How is it that men make oxen run by setting their tails on
fire,[40]
Entice horses by faraway mares in heat,
But never think of the quiet calm of their own nature?

68.

When the fish swims freely in water,
Both water and fish forget the other.[41]
When the bird rides the wind and flies far away,
It knows nothing of the wind's existence.
If you understand such things, you can transcend
external involvements,[42]
And enjoy all that Heaven performs.[43]

69.

Foxes sleep on the broken paving stones,
Rabbits run through the wasted tower;
Here was, in years long past, a place of dances and song.
The dew chills the chrysanthemums,
The mists become lost in the dried-up grass;
Everything here, in times long ago, was witness to war.
Prosperity and decline, how long can they continue?
Strength and weakness, can either last for long?
Thinking of this, my heart turns to ashes.

70.

Do not be surprised by either praise or blame;
Look peacefully in the garden as flowers bloom and
flowers fall.
Give no regard to either leaving or staying;
Ramble along after the sky as clouds fold up and clouds
stretch away.

71.

Under a clear sky and bright moon,
How many should be flitting free under the heavens:
Flying moths that hurl themselves into night lanterns
all alone?
With clear springs and green grasses,
How many other morsels should they able to peck at and
eat:
The owls that so love the rotted flesh of mice?[44]
Ahh, those people in this world who do not resemble the
moths and owls,
How many can there be?

72.

After finally boarding the raft,
        to then think about tossing it away:
    This is surely an unobstructed Man of the Way.
After mounting the donkey,[45]
        to then go out in its search:
    This is, for certain, the Zen Master without a clue.

73.

The powerful and elite clash like dragons;
The brave and manly fight like tigers.
If you look at this with a cool and reasoned eye,
    It is like ants gathering at the smell of fish,
    Or flies vying over blood.
They swarm like hornets over right and wrong;
They bristle like hedgehogs over gain and loss.
If you handle this with a cool and reasoned mind,
    It is like changing metal in a cast,
    Like melting snow with hot water.

74.

If you're bridled and chained by worldly desire,
You will learn how distressful life can be.
If you're comfortable and at ease with your own true nature,
You will learn how life can be enjoyed.
Knowing how you become distressed,
Your earthly desires will be destroyed;
Knowing how life can be enjoyed,
You will, of yourself, reach the mind of the sage.

75.

When every sliver of earthly desire has left your breast,
It will be like snow melted by the flames of a kiln, or ice melted by the sun.
When the full clarity of the firmament opens before your eyes,
The moon will always be in an azure sky, its reflection always on the waves.

76.

The inspiration of poetry resides on the bridge at Pa.[46]
    When singing the poems to yourself,
    Forests and crags will be spacious and vast.
The inspiration of the rustic ideal lives in places like
        Lake Chien.[47]
    When walking along alone,
    Mountains and rivers reflect each other naturally.

77.

The bird that rests long will surely fly high;
The flower that blooms first departs swiftly and alone.
Knowing that,
    You can avoid the misery of dragging your feet;
    You can extinguish thoughts of impatience and haste.

78.

When trees and shrubs return to their roots,
    They know the passing glory
        of flowers, blooms, shoots, and leaves.
When human affairs are encased in the grave,[48]
    One knows the futility
        of wife and child, jewels and brocades.

79.

The True Void is not Void,
Attachment to phenomena is not Truth;
    But breaking through phenomena is also not Truth.
You ask:
What did the Buddha say about this?
    "Exist in the world, but transcend it."
Following desires is bitterness,
But suppressing desires is the same.
This is what follows from all of our disciplines.

80.

The gallant man will decline a fief of a thousand chariots;
The miser will fight over a penny.
    Their characters are as different as the stars and the
        abyss,
    But loving fame differs not a whit from loving profit.
The emperor manages the affairs of the state;
The beggar cries out for a cooked morsel or two.
    Their positions are as different as Heaven and Earth,
    But how does scorching the mind differ from
        scorching the voice?

81.

Once you sample enough of the world's piquancy,
You accept that human emotions may shift from rain to
clouds with the flick of the wrist
And resist even opening your eyes.
Once you understand the nature of man,
You let yourself be called a cow or a horse,
And simply nod your head in assent.[49]

82.

People today seek only No-Mind,
But their minds, in the end, cannot attain Emptiness.
Simply do not be tied down by previous thoughts,[50]
Do not go out to greet thoughts that come after.
Only in taking care of things as they appear
From their present cause and effect
Do you naturally and gradually enter the Void.

83.

Where your mind is suddenly delighted,
There significance will be;[51]
Where things have come from nature,
You will see true charm.
Where even a portion has been interposed or arranged,
Its flavor quickly declines!
Po Chu-i[52] said,
The mind is at peace when without events;
The wind is clear when it gathers of its own.
Do these not contain true flavor, these words?

84.

If your original nature has become clear,
Though you simply eat when hungry and drink when thirsty,
You will not be without peace and salvation for body and mind.
If your mind has become sunken and confused,
Though you expound Zen doctrine and chant the sutras,
All will be playing and trifling with both spirit and soul.

85.

In the human heart there is a place of Truth:
Even without stringed instruments or flutes,[53]
    It will, of itself, experience a peaceful joy;
Even without incense or tea,
    It will, of itself, have a clear fragrance.
Thus, make your heart pure and your mind empty;
Forget ruminations and disregard material form.
Only so encircled can you wander as you please.

86.

Gold is taken from ore;
Gems are produced from stone.
    Without illusion, there would be no seeking after
        Truth.
The Way may be obtained within one's cups;[54]
The land of enchantment met within the blossoms.[55]
    Although refinement exists, we cannot part from the
        mundane.

87.

The Ten Thousand Things between Heaven and Earth,
The myriad emotions of human relations,
The countless events in the midst of the world:
    When you observe them with the common eye,
    They are all in confusion, each different from the other.
    When you penetrate them with the eye of the Way,
    Their infinite variety is always the same.
Why go to the trouble of making distinctions?
Why go to the expense of picking and choosing?

88.

If the spirit is in full bloom,
    Though you inhabit a room wearing only rough clothes,
You will obtain the harmonious energy of the universe.
If what you taste is satisfactory,
    Though you drink only goosefoot soup,
You will know the true piquancy of human simplicity.

89.

Whether shackled or free, you have but one mind.
If it is a mind of understanding,
Then butcher stores and wine shops are paradise just as
        they are.

But if the mind is not so,
  Though you play the lute and raise cranes,
  Though you cultivate flowers and plant grasses,
  Though your tastes and pleasures are pure,
The goblin of interference will still be there.
As the saying goes:[56]
  If you are capable of tranquility, the world of dust
    becomes the world of truth;
  If you have not yet understood, a monk is nothing
    more than a vulgar man on the street.[57]
Is this not true?

90.

If, in a room as small as a box,
You toss away all of your ten thousand thoughts,
Will you not enjoy the clouds that pass by painted eaves
  And the rain that falls by the bound jeweled blind?
If, after three cups of wine,[58]
The One Truth is, of itself, obtained,
You will perfectly know how to play
  An unadorned lute under the moon.

91.

When all the world's sounds are silent and at peace,
    And you suddenly hear the playful voice of a single bird,
Numerous aspects of the Mysterious are evoked.
After all the world's grasses have withered and died,
    And you suddenly see a single branch
        eclipse the others and bloom,
The limitlessness of life's forces is clearly felt.
Thus we understand,
    The Original Nature does not dry up forever;
    The vigor of the spirit, you should touch and unfold.

92.

Po Chu-i said,
    You should let go of body and mind, and entrust
        things unseen to the working of nature.
Chao Pu-chih[59] said,
    You should discipline body and mind, and return
        them encased to peace and regulation.
Letting go too far results in insanity,
But too much discipline leads to a withering of the self.
Only the man who directs his body and mind well
    Can hold the hilt of the sword and leave discipline and
        its lack
    To their own.

93.

On a snowbound, moonlit night,
    The mind echoes the same clarity and purity.
With a tranquil and mild spring breeze,
    Feelings are softened and melt on their own.
Nature and Man's mind
Blend and mix, with no margin between.

94.

Literature advances by way of the inexpert;
The Way develops by the same means.
But the word *inexpert* has limitless meaning.
Sentences like
    The dogs barking at Peach Blossom Spring, or
    The rooster crowing amidst the mulberry trees,[60]
Are gentle and replete.
But to write something like
    The moon over the cold pool, or
    A crow on a withered branch,
Within the works of technique alone,
We feel a disposition lacking in life.

95.

If you can employ the external world[61]
In obtaining, you will not rejoice;
In loss, you will not despair.
You will travel free and easy no matter where you go.
If you are employed by the external,
In reverses, you'll engender enmity;
In favorable conditions, you'll become attached.
Thus, even something as small as a hair becomes fetters and chains.

96.

When principle is at peace, phenomena will be at peace.
But disregarding phenomena and grasping at principle
Resembles letting the shadow go, and leaving only the form.
If the mind is empty, externals will be empty.
But letting go of externals and retaining only the mind
Is like piling up raw meat, and trying to drive away the flies.

97.

The artistic actions of mountain hermits
  Are appropriate for who they are.[62]
Thus, wine is enjoyed without making it too strong,
Go is played best without bruising competition,
The flute is timely when played without meter,
The lute is most refined when played without strings,
Meeting others is truly sincere when dates have not been set,
  And guests are at ease when not being greeted or sent off.
If you are once caught up by pattern, or mired down in convention,
  You will fall into the dust of the world, into a bitter sea.

98.

Trying to imagine what form you had before you were born[63]
  And what one you will take long after you have died,
Your myriad thoughts will turn to cold ashes,
Your true nature will stand alone,
You will naturally transcend the external world,
  And you will be at ease in a world beyond appearances.

99.

Thinking about the jewel of strength after becoming sick;
Ruminating on the good fortune of peace after
        encountering trouble—
    These are not instances of foresight.
Knowing beforehand that accepting a windfall is the basis
        of disaster;
Realizing in advance that coveting life is the cause of
        death—
    These are examples of superior intelligence.

100.

The actress puts on white powder and
        daubs herself with rouge,
    And with the touch of the brush creates
        both beauty and crone.
But when the songs have been sung and
        the theater is closed,
    Where are beauty and crone then?
The *go* player fights for the fore and contends for the rear,
    Competes with each stone for victory or defeat.
But when the game has ended and the stones are put away,
    Where are victory and defeat then?

101.

The exquisite beauty of breeze and blossoms,
The refreshing clarity of moon and snow—
Only the tranquil man can enjoy them as a master.
The flourishing and withering of the waters and woods,
The growth and decline of the rocks[64] and bamboo—
Only the man at peace can enjoy them as a lord.

102.

An old man from the country or fields,
In talk about roast fowl or unrefined wine,
He will be cheerful and pleased.
But ask about aristocratic kettles and urns,
And of this he knows nothing at all.
In talk about hand-me-downs or old padded clothes,
He will be open and gay.
But ask about ceremonial robes and cloaks,
And of these he will not have a clue.
His nature is intact,
And thus his desires are plain.
This, indeed, is man's highest condition.

103.

The True Mind is free from distracting thoughts,
So why should we look into it?
  Shakamuni's comment that we should observe the
    Mind
  Only heaps up obstructions.
All things originally being One,
Why should we have them be equal?
  Chuang Tzu's comment about the equality of all things
  Itself divides their uniformity.

104.

Just when the flutes and songs are at their most buoyant,
He gathers his belongings, and leaves for someplace far
    away—
  How enviable, this accomplished man's strolling freely
    along the precipice.
After the clocks have all run out,
He unsteadily walks through the night without rest—
  How laughable, this vulgar man's sinking himself
    in a bitter sea.

105.

While you have not yet disciplined yourself,
It is best not to take steps into the world of dust and din,
Nor to expose the mind to desirable things and then to confusion.
Thus you keep pure the self's peaceful substance.
When self-control is firm,
Then you are ready to mix your steps with the world's wind and grit,
To let your heart see what is tempting and yet not be confounded.
Thus you sustain the self's versatility and grace.

106.

He who rejoices in quiet and shrinks from noise
Will sometimes avoid others and seek peace.
He does not know that
With his intention of being where men are not, he engenders the concept of self;
With a mind attached to peace, he establishes the root of activity.
How about reaching the point
Where self and other are regarded as one,
And activity and peace are both forgotten?

107.

Living in the mountains, the breast is clear and pure;
Whatever you touch has its own excellence.
    Watching a wisp of cloud or a crane in a field[65]
    Wakes your thoughts to transcendence.

Being among scattered rocks and flowing springs
Moves the mind to purification.
    Gently touching the old cypress or the cold plum tree,
    A sense of integrity is drawn out.
Accompanying the sea gull and the deer,[66]
The conniving heart is quickly forgotten.

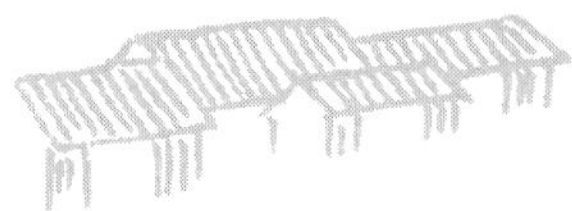

    But once the city's dust is entered again,
    Even the things with which you have no ties
    Surround you and pull you down.

108.

When my inclinations are in harmony with the moment,
    Shoeless, I walk leisurely through fragrant grasses.
Then the birds put off their scolding and become, at
        times, my friends.
When my surroundings are in accord with my mind,
    I loosen my collar and sit at ease beneath falling
        blossoms,
Then the silent white clouds approach unperceived and
        remain at my side.

109.

Life's fortunes and misfortunes—
All are produced by the functions of the mind.
For this reason Shakamuni said,
    When the desire for gain burns brightly,
    It is nothing other than the fires of hell.
    When you are sunk in avarice and greed,
    You will surely swim in bitter seas.
    But if you are determined to be pure,
    Raging flames become cool lake waters;
    If you are determined to be enlightened,
    The boat will reach the other side.[67]
When the mind changes just a little,
The world quickly becomes different, too.
Is this not true?

110.

A rope pulled back and forth eventually cuts through
        wood;
    Water dropped bit by bit in time wears through stone.[68]
Studying the Way, increase your efforts in the search.
Flowing water in due time carves a ditch;
    The melon ripening on the vine will one day fall to the
        ground.
Obtaining the Way, leave things to the play of Heaven.

111.

When your scheming is over,
The moon comes up and the wind arrives,
And you are no longer in the bitter sea of the human world.
When the mind is far away,
And the dust of wagons or horses' tracks cannot be found,[69]
Why this chronic disease of having to be in the mountains and hills?

112.

When grasses and trees have begun to wither and fade,
Buds and sprouts appear on the roots.
Though with the order of time there is freezing and cold,
In the end spring returns with the flying ash.[70]
That there is life
In the midst of death and decline[71]
Is an eternal principle.
Thus can be seen the heart of Heaven and Earth.

113.

If you observe the color of the mountains just after the
rain,
You are aware that scenery is fresh and beautiful.
If you hear the sound of the bell in the evening stillness,
You feel its reverberations to be all the more serene and
clear.

114.

Climbing to high elevations makes the heart expansive;
Looking out on flowing waters takes your thoughts far
away.[72]
Reading books on a night of snow or rain
Purifies the spirit.
Leisurely singing some lines at the crest of a hill
Makes your inspiration soar.

115.

When your mind is expansive, even the highest salary
is like an unglazed jug.
When your mind is narrow, even a single hair
has the girth of a wagon wheel.

116.

If there were no wind, moon, flowers, or willows,
    Nature itself would have no form.
If there were no emotions, desires, predilections, or tastes,
    The mind itself would remain unformed.
Only with the man who controls externals
And who is not controlled by externals himself,
Are predilections and desires not separate from Nature's
        play,
Is the dust of emotions nothing other than the Truth.

117.

When you have come to an understanding of yourself,
    You can, for the first time, let the world take care
        of its own.
When you return all under Heaven to itself,
    You can, right now, transcend society without leaving
        it at all.

118.

If a man's life contains excessive leisure,
Worldly thoughts will surreptitiously arise.
If there is excessive occupation,
His true character will not become manifest.
Therefore, the gentleman
Cannot but embrace the troubles
of both body and mind,
Yet must be steeped in the pleasures
of wind and moon.

119.

Many times the Truth is lost from the oscillation of the
human heart.
But if you refuse to let a single thought be born
And meditate with a settled mind,
You will leisurely move on with the rising clouds,
Be purified in the chill of the falling rain,
Be cheerfully satisfied with the singing birds,
And wholly understand yourself with the falling
flowers.
In what place will Truth not exist?
In what thing will Truth not move?

120.

When a child is born, the mother is in danger; when
        money is amassed,
    Thieves await their chance.
    What joy, then, cannot become a sorrow?
Because of poverty, we use thrift; because of illness,
    We take care of our health.
    What sorrow, then, cannot become a joy?
Therefore, the man of attainment
    Regards prosperity and reversal as the same,
    And forgets both joy and sorrow.

121.

Our sense of hearing resembles a whirlwind hurling itself
        down the valley:
    If it passes on without lingering,
    Both good and evil will go with it.
Our mind is like the moon submerging its colors in a pool:
    If it is empty and unattached,
    It will forget both self and the outside world.

122.

People of this world wrap themselves in chains
For the sake of profit and gain,
Then talk of the world of dust, the sea of bitterness.
They do not know that
Clouds are white, mountains blue.
Rivers run, rocks stand tall.
Blossoms invite, birds laugh.
The valley responds, the woodcutters sing.
This world, after all, is not of dust;
The sea, after all, is not bitter.
It is only that, on their own, people put dust and
bitterness in their hearts.

123.

Viewing flowers in partial bloom,
Drinking wine to only mild inebriation—
Within such things there is a strong sense of
refinement.
But if you only treasure full bloom
Or drink until you fall down drunk,
You enter evil territory.
The man who strides toward saturation
Should think this over more than once.

124.

Mountain vegetables[73] will not thrive under cultivation
 or manmade compost;
Birds of the field will not respond to human nurturing
 and care.
 The taste of such things is savory and fresh.
If we human beings were able to remain untainted by
 greed and fame,
Our dispositions would likely have similar qualities.

125.

Planting flowers, raising bamboo,
Taking pleasure in cranes, observing fish—
 Still, you need a bit of self-understanding.
When you are vainly addicted to the scenery before you,
Or take pleasure only in the external environment,
It is what the Confucians call
 Learning that comes in the ears
 And goes right out the mouth.[74]
Or what the Buddhist call
 Obstinately grasping the void.
What kind of refinement is this?

126.

Recluses living in mountains and forests practice pure poverty,
But their transcendence is of itself abundant.
Men toiling on the farms and in the fields are vulgar and plain,
But possess a natural sincerity that is complete.
Even once losing yourself to the brokers of village and town[75]
Does not equal falling to your death in a ravine and leaving behind a pure body and soul.

127.

Fortune beyond your status,
Things entrusted to you for no reason—
If these are not snares set by the Creator of Things,
They are traps laid by the world at large.
With such encounters, if you do not fix your eyes high,
You will rarely fail to fall for their tricks.

128.

The human is, at bottom, nothing more than a
marionette.
You need only to have your hands at the source
To let no string become tangled,
To pull and release each freely,
To have *stop* and *go* reside in yourself,
And not to allow even a thin hair to be manipulated by
another.
In this way, you can surely transcend this place.

129.

When one event takes place, one injury will surely follow.
Therefore, in this world it has always been that
happiness
Arises from the lack of events.
If you read the poetry of a man of earlier times,[76]
you will find this:
I advise you, friend, do not talk of
appointments and fiefs.
The fame of one general is built from the
bones of ten thousand.
It is also said that[77]
In the world forever move all things toward peace.

Then famous swords may rust in their boxes for ten thousand years without regret.
Thus, though one may be ambitious and wild,
He will, unawares, melt away like ice and sleet.

130.

A lascivious woman in her extremity
Will become a nun.
A hot-blooded man in his exasperation
Will enter the Buddhist Way.
Thus the gates to purity and ablution[78]
Are forever the haunts and lairs of the licentious and lewd.

131.

When surging waves reach the heavens,
Those aboard a ship have no sense of fear,
While those not on the ship are struck cold with terror.
When a howling drunk rails against friends seated with him,
Those at the table pay him no mind,
While those at a distance bite their tongues in disgust.
Therefore, the gentleman,
Though sailing bodily amidst events,
Should pass far beyond them in his mind.

132.

When you decrease or curtail some things a bit,
Life is transcended by the same amount.
If meetings with friends are decreased, confusion is
avoided.
If words and utterances are decreased, errors are greatly
reduced.
If thoughts and reflections are decreased, the spirit is not
dissipated.
If cleverness is decreased, the Great Nebulous[79] can be
brought to perfection.
Those who seek daily not to decrease, but to add,
Truly bring to their lives fetters and chains.[80]

133.

The heat and cold of Heaven's revolutions are easy to
avoid;
The flames and frigidity of society are difficult to elude.
Even if the flames and frigidity of society are easy to
elude,
The freezing and charring of your mind are
difficult to remove.
If you are able to remove the freezing
and charring from within,

All within your breast will be in harmony:
Wherever you go, spring breezes will follow of themselves.

134.

I do not wish for the finest tea, but the jar is never empty.
I do not ask for the purest wines, but the cask is never dry.
My plain lute is without strings, but always in tune.
My short flute is not hollow, but is just right for itself.
Though it would be difficult to play as well as
Emperor Hsi,[81]
I can count myself an equal to Chi and Yuan.[82]

135.

Shakamuni's "Following one's karma";
Our Confucian "Adapting to one's position"[83]—
These two phrases are the water wings you may use
to cross the sea.
The world's road is wide.
If you have even a single thought of seeking total
satisfaction,
Every possible desire will leap up in confusion.
Be at ease following your temporary circumstances,
And there will be no situation where you cannot
yourself be.

AFTERWORD

East of the Kamo River in the city of Kyoto is the Kennin-ji, the first Zen temple in the ancient capital. Established in 1202 by the priest Eisai (1141–1215), it was a temple first for the study of Shingon, Tendai, and Zen Buddhism, but soon after exclusively for the latter. Like many other temples in Japan, it is the repository of a number of national art treasures, among them the works by the great painters Kaiho Yusho and Tawaraya Sotatsu. In many cases, such cultural objects are displayed only once or twice a year, and then carefully stored away.

The Kennin-ji has some fourteen subtemples in its precincts, and one of these—the Ryosoku-in—possesses a treasure of its own. This is a painting by a certain Josetsu[1] that depicts the patriarchs of the Three Creeds; that is, Confucianism, Buddhism, and Taoism (see page 30). The brushwork, astonishing in its strength and decisiveness, portrays Lao Tzu with an amused but solid grin, and the Buddha as though he had just had a good laugh at some outrageous joke. On Confucius, the upturned corners of what might otherwise be considered a grimace, seem to indicate that he is just barely controlling himself over some bit of hilarity. The message is clear: these three—though quite different in personality—are having a good time together and are enjoying each other's company. The overall impression is that there is no contention whatsoever among them.

This is a fascinating artistic rendering of the doctrine of the Unity of the Three Creeds, a concept popular in China and Japan—usually among the literati—at various points in their histories. This doctrine basically finds that the three creeds or philosophies all bring fulfillment to the minds of men and lead them to the Tao. Contentions among the three are in the misunderstandings and petty prejudices of man, and not in the creeds themselves. If you choose and follow one of them, that is your own path, but that choice does not negate the other two; a path's limitations are only a matter of our own deficiencies. In fact, each creed contains gems that we can make treasures of our own.

NOTES

All quotes from the Chinese classics cited in these endnotes were translated from the original Chinese texts, found in Japanese works on those texts. The Japanese have been serious students of the Chinese classics since the sixth century A.D., and have produced some of the most scholarly works on them in the Far East. These works invariably include the original Chinese text, a Japanese reading of that text, and a clear exegesis of archaic vocabulary, grammar, and general meaning. All works cited in the bibliography follow that paradigm.

INTRODUCTION

1 Liu, *The Art of Chinese Poetry*, pg. 22.

2 Although the Yuan Dynasty (1280–1368) was headed by Mongols, it employed a cosmopolitan staff of Turks, Arabs, Jews, Italians, Uighurs, and many other foreigners as generals, architects, doctors, chroniclers, merchants, and advisers. From early on, the khans consulted Chinese Taoists, Tibetan Buddhists, Nestorian Christians, and Central Asian Muslims on both religious and secular affairs.

3 The Tung-lin Academy in particular was opposed to Wang's views, and viewed the syncretism of the late 16th century with alarm. The members of this academy were concerned with the reestablishment of clear boundaries between right and wrong, and the continuance of the social moral struggle, which they felt were being abandoned by the "extremists" of Wang Yang-ming's group in their search for personal enlightenment, or by such syncretists as the adherents of "Wildcat Zen."

4 Hung Ying-ming, 洪応明. In some texts he is cited as Hung Tzu-ch'eng, 洪自誠.

5 For more on this subject, see Prof. James Liu's *Chinese Theories of Literature*.

6 Liu, *The Art of Chinese Poetry*, pg. 85.

A PREFATORY VERSE

1 Also referred to as the Confucian Five Classics. They are the *I Ching* or the *Book of Changes*, the *Shu Ching* or the *Book of History*, the

Shih Ching or the *Book of Odes* (or the *Book of Poetry*), the *Li Chi* or the *Book of Rites*, and the *Ch'un-ch'iu* or the *Spring and Autumn Annals*. These were books that Confucius felt to be the backbone of Chinese culture and civilization. None were written by him, although it is said that he edited the *Book of Odes* and wrote commentary on the *I Ching*, which are now incorporated in most editions as part and parcel of the book.

2 Book I, verse 90, with a slight variation in the last line.

BOOK I

1 The man of tricks and schemes will inevitably become a man with secrets. A man with secrets will inevitably become a man of deceptions. If deceptions live in a man's breast, he will not be equipped with a pure heart. If a man is not equipped with a pure heart, his spirit will be unsettled. If a man has an unsettled spirit, he will not be able to mount the Way. It is not that I don't know about such things, but I would be ashamed to do them.

—*Chuang Tzu* (Book by a writer of the same name. Mostly fables and anecdotes, and the second most important book in the Taoist canon. 4th or 3rd century B.C.)

2 Tze Kung said, "Here there is a beautiful jewel. Should it concealed in a chest and stored away, or should we look for a good buyer and sell it?"

Confucius said, "Sell it! Sell it! I've been waiting for someone to buy it."

—*Analects* of Confucius (Known as *Lun Yu* in Chinese, and the fundamental source of Confucian thinking. 4th or 5th century B.C.)

Gold is stashed in the mountains; jewels are stashed in the abyss.

—*Chuang Tzu*

3 The Way of the holy man is to run from wisdom and artfulness. If he does not avoid wisdom and artfulness, it will be hard to establish the eternal. If the common people use such things, their personal disasters will be numerous; if a man in charge uses such things, his kingdom will fall.

—*Han Fei Tzu* (Book by a "legalist" philosopher of the same name. Died c. 233 B.C.)

4 Good medicine may lie bitter on the tongue, but it will have an effect on the disease. Loyal words may burn the ears, but they will have an effect on behavior.

—*Shuo Yuan* (A collection of biographies and anecdotes concerning famous people from the Spring and Autumn period to the early Han. By Liu Hsiang, a Han-period writer.)

5 The man who has arrived is not self-centered; the holy man is artless; the sage is without fame.

—*Chuang Tzu*

6 Change does not think and does not act. It is peaceful and does not move. It feels, and at length pierces

the world's phenomena.

—*I Ching (*Ancient book of divination and philosophy, outlining a well-ordered and dynamic universe by means of 64 hexagrams. Possibly 11th century B.C.)

7 The Way of Heaven and Earth is to reflect upon itself with constancy. The Way of the sun and the moon is to shine with constancy.

—*I Ching*

8 Mi Tzu's behavior had not changed from the outset. The act that he was praised for as a wise man at first became the crime he was charged for later because [his lord's] love had turned to hate.

—*Han Fei Tzu*

With a turn of your hand, it is cloudy;
Turn it again and it rains.
How can you account for so much
Of the ambiguous and fickle?

—Tu Fu (Chinese poet, 712–70 A.D.)

9 When you go, don't rely on narrow pathways.

—*Analects*

10 Avoid knowledge and cunning; follow the Principle of Heaven. If you do so, you will have no natural disasters, no external afflictions, no accusations from others, and no punishment from the supernatural.

—*Chuang Tzu*

11 All I ask is for mulberry and hemp,
To have the silkworms spinning under the moon.
The correct heart of artlessness is just like this,
Entering the small path I face plum, bamboo, and stone.

—Tao Yuan-ming (Chinese naturalist poet, 365–427 A.D.)

12 Thus I have written six *gathas*, and recite them on my knees in front of the Buddhist monks; and by the karma I create, hope that this will be a preliminary to entering the next world.

—Po Chu-i (Chinese poet, 772–846 A.D.)

13 His strength could pull the very mountains; his *ch'i* could shake the world.

—*Shih Chi* (*Records of the Grand Historian*. A record of China and all people known to the Chinese up to the 1st century B.C. By Ssu-ma Ch'ien, 145–90 B.C.)

14 The creator of all things: his art is mysterious, his deeds deep. From the very beginning he was difficult to fathom and difficult to sum up.

—*Lieh Tzu* (Taoist anecdotes along the line of the *Chuang Tzu*. Attributed to Lieh Yu-k'ou, 450–375 B.C.)

15 The Way of Heaven descends, and makes things bright and clear; the Way of Earth is low, but moves upward. The Way of Heaven decreases that which is full, but adds to that which is modest; the Way of Earth changes that which is full and flows toward that which is modest. The gods and demons bring harm to that which is full, but bring good fortune to that which is modest. The Way of man is to despise that which is full and

to love that which is modest.
—*I Ching*

16 Nan-guo Tzu-ch'i was seated, leaning on his armrest. Gazing up at heaven, he sighed. He seemed so empty that he looked like he might well have lost his own body. Yen-ch'eng Tzu-yu stood up in front of him awaiting his instructions, and said, "What's going on here? Can you truly make your body like a withered tree, and your mind like dead ashes?"
—*Chuang Tzu*

17 He who moves, loves moving water,
He who is still, loves water that is still.
—Po Chu-i

18 Clouds and thunder mean impairment;
The gentleman tends to the administration of the state.
—*I Ching*

19 Do not forget the beginner's mind. Do not forget the beginner's mind of right and wrong [or existence and nonexistence]. Do not forget the everyday beginner's mind. Do not forget the beginner's mind of old age.
—Zeami (1363–1443 Considered to be father of the classical Japanese drama, Noh. Well acquainted with classic texts of both China and Japan, as well as sutras and lore of Zen Buddhism.)

20 Attain complete emptiness, observe a deliberate peace. All creatures are brought into being one after another; but with this, I perceive their return [to the Tao].
—*Tao Te Ching* (The most fundamental Taoist work; in maxims, verse, and prose. Traditionally considered to be written by Lao Tzu, 6th century B.C.)

21 Superior virtue is not the virtue you think of; therefore it is virtuous. Inferior virtue is the virtue to which you hold on tight; therefore it is not virtuous. Superior virtue is that of not-doing; so, by doing nothing, you do it. Inferior virtue is something you do; so, by doing it, it's out there in front . . . Therefore, when the Way is lost, virtue raises its [ugly] head.
—*Tao Te Ching*

22 It is easy to destroy the insurgents in the mountains. It is difficult to destroy the insurgents in the mind.
—Wang Yang-ming (Philosopher, statesman, and general. A Confucian influenced by Zen Buddhism. 1472–1529 A.D.)

23 If men concentrated their will, they would have more command of their *ch'i*. If they concentrated their *ch'i*, they would have more command of their will.
—*Mencius* (Book by author of same name, 371–289 B.C. Also *Meng Tzu*. Second to Confucius as a Confucian philosopher.)

24 The ram is caught in the hedge;
It can neither retreat nor go forward./There is no place to make gain,/Nor any way to good fortune.
—*I Ching*.

25 Literally, *square*.

26 Literally, *round*.

27 Rites are something created by vulgar society. Truth is something received from Heaven; it is Of-Itself-So, and does not change. Thus, the sage governs himself according to Heaven, and respects truth. He is not influenced by the vulgar.
—*Chuang Tzu*

28 According to Neo-Confucianism, the man in harmony with the universe not only receives life but helps the life of the universe along as well.

29 The absolutely straight looks crooked; great skill looks inept; real eloquence sounds like stuttering.
—*Tao Te Ching*

30 Confucius saw that there was a top-heavy bottle at the court of Prince Huan of Lu. When he asked a guard at the door, "What kind of bottle is this?" the guard replied, "This is a vessel always to be kept at one's side." Confucius said, "I have heard that when this bottle is empty, it lies on its side; when half full, it stands correctly; when completely full, it turns upside down." Confucius thought about this and said to his disciple, "Pour in some water." The disciple took some water and poured it in. When the bottle was half full, it stood correctly; but when full, it turned upside down; when empty, it lay on its side. Confucius sank into dejection and lamented, "Aah, why are there still those who when full do not turn upside down?'"
—*Hsun Tzu* (Book of early Chinese legalism by author of the same name, 298–238 B.C.)

31 Confucius said, "How praiseworthy is Hui: One reed tray for his food, one gourd for his drink, living in a back alley. People can't bear up under such affliction, but Hui does nothing to improve the pleasure [he gets regardless]."
—*Analects*

32 In the *Shu Ching* it says, "When you are at ease, think of danger." If you think things over, you will be prepared; if you are prepared, there will be no disasters.
—*Tso Chuan* (Commentary on the *Spring and Autumn Annals,* covering the years 472–468 B.C. A combination of history and philosophy, said to be compiled in the 3rd century B.C. by Ts'o Ch'iu-ming.)

33 The sage is not stagnant or clinging to things,
But is able to change the world.
—*Ch'u Tz'u* (*Elegies of Ch'u*. A book of poetry from the southern area of China, attributed to Ch'u Yuan, 329–299 B.C.)

34 Listen, the coming of disasters is given birth by man himself, and the coming of good fortune is created by man on his own. Disaster and good fortune come through the same gate, and advantage and harm are neighbors. But if you're not a sage, you won't understand this well.
—*Huai Nan Tzu*

35 Since times past, if a man does some-

thing great but does not step aside, complaints have rained down.

—Li Pai (Chinese poet, 701–62)

36 The person whose filial piety is deep and loving will undoubtedly have a friendly spirit. The person who has a friendly spirit will undoubtedly have a happy disposition.

—*Li Chi* (*Book of Rites*. 1st-century-B.C. compilation of Chou-Dynasty rituals and regulations. One of the Confucian classics.)

37 Now listen, by riding the wave of things, you make your mind free and easy; by going along with what can't be helped and nourishing your core—that's the greatest!

—*Chuang Tzu*

38 The ear stops with hearing; the mind stops with cognizance. The spirit, however, is something that, when void, will contain anything. Only the Way gathers the void. The void is the mind's purification.

—*Chuang Tzu*

39 If the water is quite clear, there will be no fish; if you govern people too closely, you will have no followers.

—*K'ung Tzu Chia Yu* (*The House Records of Confucius.* Apocryphal work concerning the words and deeds of Confucius, and questions and answers to his disciples. Attributed to Wang Su of the Wei period, 220–264.)

40 Therefore, the sages said that he who takes on the disgrace of his country is called the master of the land.

—*Tao Te Ching*

It is Heaven's Way that rivers and ponds wash away dirt, the mountains and thickets keep poisonous insects, that beautiful jewels conceal their flaws, and that the lord of the land harbors its disgrace.

—*Tso Chuan*

41 Now when the Great Caster molds metal, and the metal leaps out and says, "I must be made into the greatest of swords," the Caster will likely consider the metal to be ill-omened. Now if there is a substance to be used for a human form, and it says, "I must only be made into a human, only a human," the Creator of Things is likely to consider it an ill-omened being.

—*Chuang Tzu*

42 Chen Pai-sha, 1428–99.

43 Meaning "The True Mind."
The Abbot of Yen, Shui Yen, used to call out to himself every day, "Old Man who is Master!" Then he would respond to himself, "Yes?" Thereupon he would say, "Be enlightened! Be enlightened!" "Right!" "From here on out, don't be fooled by others!" "Right! Right!"

—*Wu Men Kuan* (*The Gateless Gate*. A collection of Zen koans compiled by the Zen master Wu-men Hui-k'ai, 1183–1260.)

44 The accomplished man uses his mind like a mirror: he neither pulls nor pushes; he responds but does not hold. Thus he is able to bear things but not harm them.

—*Chuang Tzu*

45 After putting the lid on a man's

casket, for the first time his affairs are confirmed. You, My Lord, are happily still not among the elderly.

—Tu Fu

46 Blessings for the people are, on the exterior, that their lord possesses the Way; and on the interior, that neighboring enemies bear no grudges.

—*Han Fei Tzu*

47 In a house where there is an accumulation of good, there will invariably be an abundance of happiness.
In a house where there is an accumulation of evil, there will invariably be an abundance of disasters.

—*I Ching*

48 With a *yangch'i* (陽氣—cheerfulness, vivacity), you can penetrate metal and stone. With a concentration of spirit, there should be nothing you can't do.

—*Chu Hsi Yu Lui* (The sayings of the Confucian scholar Chu Hsi, 1130–1200.)

49 It is as if the True Master were there, but you cannot find his tracks.

—*Chuang Tzu*

50 Shun said, "If my body is not my own possession, whose is it?" He said, "This is the form entrusted to us by Heaven and Earth."

—*Chuang Tzu*

51 Heaven and Earth called me into existence, and I am one with the Ten Thousand Things.

—*Chuang Tzu*

52 Release your body from the troubles of its chains;
Remove your ears from the morning's noise.

—Po Chu-i

53 The five colors will make the eyes blind,
The five sounds will make the ears deaf,
The five tastes will give the mouth a sweet tooth.

—*Tao Te Ching*

54 Savory tastes rot the stomach;
Lovely sounds confuse the mind.

—*Lun Heng* (*Critical Essays*. Essays to clarify true Confucianism, written by Wang Ch'ung, 27–97 A.D.)

55 Pei-i and Shu-ch'i did not dwell on old hatreds. They had rare use to hold a grudge.

—*Analects*

56 Someone said, "Returning hostility with kindness; how about this?" Confucius replied, "How then will you repay kindness? Repay hostility with directness; repay kindness with kindness."

—*Analects*

57 Youth is defined as thirty.

—*Li Chi*

58 You should be able to run away from disasters made by Heaven, but you cannot flee those you have made yourself.

—*Shu Ching* (*Book of Documents*. The first work of Chinese history, traditionally held to be compiled by Confucius.)

59 Great apprehension is like approaching a deep pond or treading on thin ice.

—*Shih Ching* (*Book of Odes*.

305 songs compiled around 600 B.C. Highly valued by Confucius.)

60 Listen, the man of secret virtue will invariably have clearly manifested rewards; the man of secret [good] acts, a bright reputation.
—*Huai Nan Tzu*

61 The virtue of a single meal will invariably be rewarded; the grudge from a hateful glare will invariably reap its own return.
—*Shih Chi*

62 Great skill looks like ineptitude.
—*Tao Te Ching*

63 The gentleman, while in public, uses the dark but remains bright.
—*I Ching*

64 The inchworm's bending is how it seeks to extend.
—*I Ching*

65 If your boat is lost in the middle of the river, a tub is worth a thousand in cash.
—*Ho Kuan Tzu* (Taoist book by unknown author.)

66 A rigid integrity should not be constant.
—*I Ching*

67 When indecision comes and goes,
Friends will follow your thoughts.
—*I Ching*

68 Looking deeply into the room where you live, do not feel ashamed of its deep recesses.
—*Shih Ching*

69 When the people of the world all know beauty as beauty,
There arises the recognition of ugliness.
When they all know the good as good,
There arises the recognition of evil.
—*Tao Te Ching*

70 If there is virtue, I will show friendship; if I do not criticize, there may be division and doubts.
—*Tso Chuan*

71 Good works never leave the gate;
Evil actions travel a thousand miles.
—*Pei-meng So-yen* (Sung-Dynasty book covering near-forgotten events of five generations spanning the T'ang and Sung dynasties. Written by Sun Kuang-hsien.)

72 *Wang liang* (Japanese, *moryo*) 魍魎: A special little spirit of the mountains and rivers, trees and rocks. One of its favorite games is to imitate the human voice and lead people astray.

73 When you embrace a disposition to help all things,
Do not turn your back on the impure of heart.
—Hsieh Ling-yen (Chinese poet, 384–433 A.D.)

74 The moon in the mountains I love
Shines and glows,
hanging over the scattered woods.
—Chen Shan-ming (Possibly Chinese poet. Dates unknown.)

75 I set the net for fish,
But the cygnet was caught instead.
I sought only a simple pleasure,
But obtained this old humpback.
—*Book of Poetry*

76 The virtues of the divine spirits, how they flourish! You may look

but not see them, you may listen but not hear them. They are embodied in things and cannot be discarded . . . The *Shih Ching* says, "The coming of the divine cannot be fathomed. How then can you ignore them?"

—*Chung Yung* (*Doctrine of the Mean*. One of the Confucian Four Books; a chapter of the *Li Chi*. From the more mystical wing of the Confucian doctrine.)

77 A man's work is done by the time he is seventy. If he is unable to resign [by then], it will be said that his desk has been given to him as a cane.

—*Li Chi*

78 Wang Yang-ming (1472–1528). A philosopher, general, and statesman. The storehouse symbolizes one's conscience.

79 Origin unknown.

80 There is nothing more apparent than what is hidden; nothing more vague than that which is manifest.

—*Doctrine of the Mean*

81 Literally, an unretreating wheel. They followed faithfully, turning the unretreating wheel [of the Buddhist Law].

—*Vimalakirti Sutra* (Popular Mahayana Buddhist sutra, written perhaps c. 100 A.D.)

82 A lamp put before the Buddha's image, representing the wisdom that keeps away the dark forever.

83 What in man cannot be learned or gained by conscious effort is called his character.

—*Hsun Tzu*

84 A quote from the poetry of Su Tung-p'o.

85 When Heaven and Earth come together, the sweet dew descends.

—*Tao Te Ching*

86 In ordinary words, he is trustworthy; in ordinary behavior, respectful. He blocks the twisted, and gives birth to sincerity.

—*I Ching*

87 Literally, "Search out the hilt of the sword," i.e., the essential place to grasp. For peace of mind in an emergency, one needs to know beforehand just where he can grasp the sword (of his true mind).

88 Tzu Kung asked, "Is there one word by which we might act all our lives?" Confucius said, "Wouldn't that be 'sympathy' (恕)? Whatever you would not want for yourself, do not do to others."

—*Analects*

89 In the middle of the autumn months, nourish the old and feeble, grant them a desk to lean on.

—*Li Chi*

90 The lotus flowers have faded,
And there is no end to the rain.
The chrysanthemums still remain,
And the branches live, though beset with frost.
You should write me your thoughts
On the very best scenery of the year.
The very best of all are the bitter oranges when yellow,
The tangerines when green.

—Su Tung-p'o (Chinese poet, 1037–1101)

91 Confucius said, "Clever words, a well-placed look, excessive politeness: Tso Ch'iu-ming was ashamed of these, and I'm ashamed of them, too."

—*Analects*

92 Principle (理), the ruling or fundamental laws of the universe. Usually noted in contrast to 事, the phenomena that operate on these universal principles.

93 Loose and at ease, he is human-hearted;
He enjoys himself, by himself alone.

—*Kuan Tzu* (Historical and philosophical book by 7th cent. B.C. statesman, Kuan Chung.)

94 Confucius said, "The gentleman stands in awe of three things: He stands in awe of what Heaven has decreed, he stands in awe of great men, and he stands in awe of the words of the sages. The small-minded man does not know what Heaven has decreed, and thus has no awe; he acts familiar with great men, and resents the words of the sages."

—*Analects*

95 Bearing no grudges against Heaven, nor blame against others, excelling in knowing what's close to you, and knowing yourself—is this not Heaven?

—*Analects*

96 When an emotion stirs inside, one expresses it in words; words being inadequate, one sighs over it; sighs being inadequate, one sings it in poetry; poetry being inadequate, one unconsciously dances with his hands and stamps his feet.

—*The Major Preface* in the Chinese anthology *Book of Poetry* (or *Book of Odes*, Chinese: *Shih Ching*).

97 The net exists because of the fish; when the fish is obtained, the net is forgotten. The snare exists because of the rabbit; when the rabbit is obtained, the snare is forgotten. Words exist because of meaning; when the meaning is obtained, the words are forgotten.

—*Chuang Tzu*

98 Not embracing the powerful, not embracing the high-positioned, not embracing relatives—this is friendship. For a friend, embrace that friend's virtue.

—*Mencius*

99 When you bear-hug [wealth, fame, and power], you will immediately embrace fear; when you let them go, you are sad. The person who never for a second reflects on this, but never stops oogling such things, will be cut down by Heaven.

—*Chuang Tzu*

100 The man who has arrived is not self-centered; the holy man performs no meritorious deeds; the sage is not famous.

—*Chuang Tzu*

101 Beneath Heaven, why should you be anxious, why apprehensive? All things under Heaven return to the same place; the roads they travel are different, but their arrival is one. Yet their thoughts are myriad.

Why should they be anxious, why apprehensive?
—I Ching

102 See footnote 90.

BOOK II

1 That is, the secluded country life.

2 Trees fall, rivers dry up, a thousand cliffs crumble—these, as well, I see distantly to be my unadorned self.
—Chu Hsi

3 The man who dreams of drinking wine may awake crying when the morning comes, and the man who dreams of crying may go hunting in the fields at daybreak. When in the dream, he is unaware that it is a dream. While in a dream, he may be interpreting a dream; but after he awakes, he knows that it was all a dream.
—Chuang Tzu

4 Yuan-ming did not understand rhythm, but he kept a stringless lute, and would play it every time he got drunk. In this way he conveyed his desires.
—Tao Yuan-ming Chuan

5 Happy in the affectionate talk of relatives and friends,
Taking pleasure in a lute and books,
And thus melting away one's grief.
—Tao Yuan-ming

6 石室丹丘: According to the poets, this is the land of the "mountain genies," where the sun always shines, and death has no place.

7 Areas of famous scenery in ancient China.

8 *Wei ch'en* (微塵): Literally, the smallest particle of dust, or atoms; referring to the third of the four stages of a *kalpa*, or world cycle: becoming, abiding, disintegration, and emptiness. According to Buddhist theory, after the world has formed and existed for some time, it is destroyed by fire, flood, and wind, reducing it to atoms, or the tiniest pieces of dust.

9 All phenomena are
like a dream, an apparition, a bubble
or a shadow;
They are like dew, or again, like lightning.
Hence, you should see them like this.
—Diamond Sutra (Major Mahayana Buddhist sutra, written between 2nd century B.C. and 3rd century A.D.)

10 On the snail's left horn there is a country whose inhabitants are called the Ch'u; on the snail's right horn there is a country whose inhabitants are called the Man. From time to time they fight over land, the corpses are in the tens of thousands, and while the victors chase the losers, it is half a month before they turn around.
—Chuang Tzu

What do they fight over, on the horns of the snail?
This body is like the light from the flint's spark.
Now following wealth, now following poverty,
They shortly make merry;
He who does not open his

mouth and laugh is a fool.
—Po Chu-i

11 See Book I, note 16.

12 A note in the text indicates that these lines refer, not to marriage, but euphemistically to a comfortable retiring from the world.

13 Confucius said, "To eat plain foods and drink water, to bend an elbow for a pillow: is there not also pleasure in this? But to be unrighteous and thus gain wealth and rank: I regard these just as floating clouds."
—*Analects*

14 Everyone in this world is muddied,
I, alone, am quite clear.
The masses of people are all drunk,
I, alone, am sober.
—Ch'u Yuan (Southern Chinese poet, 329–399 B.C.)

15 "This," i.e., wisdom or intellect.
When one engages himself in study, he increases daily; when he practices the Way, he decreases daily. Decrease this, and then decrease it again, and you will arrive at nonactivity. When no action is taken, nothing will be left undone.
—*Tao Te Ching*

16 Once, on the ninth day of the ninth month, Tao Yuan-ming was without wine. He went out among the chrysanthemums, picked a few, making a bundle, and sat down next to it. After a while, he noticed a man in a white robe approaching him from a distance. When the man arrived, he was bearing a gift of wine, which was immediately served.
—*T'ai P'ing Yu Lan*

17 When I contemplate those who mix with the people of today—blazing, they become attached; cold, they abandon all—there are few of this kind that perform pure deeds.
—*Liu Tsung-yuan* (Compilation of literary pieces commissioned by the Sung-Dynasty emperor in 983.)

18 See Book I, note 24.

19 If the tiger stops, the rider is likely to be eaten.

20 The person dressed in shabby padded clothes who can stand next to those adorned in robes of fox and badger skins yet feel no embarrassment—that is Yu [one of Confucius's disciples].
—*Analects*

21 White clouds embrace vague crags,
Green bamboo grass flatters the ripples.
—Hsieh Ling-yun

I divined a place to live
among piled-up crags.
Bird trails, but no sign of man.
What's in my front garden?
White clouds embracing hazy rocks.
—Han Shan (8th- or 9th-century A.D. eccentric poet. A Buddhist layman known for his poetry and unorthodox lifestyle.)

22 A cloud, with No-Mind, leaves the peaks;
Birds fly, exhausted, but know the way back home.
—Tao Yuan-ming

23 Tzu Lu said, "It damages you to be so poor. While your parents are alive, you are unable to take care of them; when they are dead, you are

unable to afford the proper ceremonies." Confucius said, "Making bean soup, drinking water, being as happy as possible: this is what is called filial piety."
—*Li Chi*

24 When hunger comes, eat your meal; when tired out, sleep. This practice alone is profound and then profound again. Don't believe what anyone else preaches; they just look for the sprites and wizards outside of the body.
—Wang Yang-ming

25 He who has used his mind to its absolute fullest, knows his own character; he who knows his own character, knows Heaven.
—*Mencius*

26 The dogs bark deep in town;
Cocks crow on the tops of the mulberry trees.
—Tao Yuan-ming

27 Take pleasure in men, and you will lose your virtue;
Take pleasure in material things, and you will lose your free will.
—*Shu Ching*

28 *Gatha*: A hymn of praise to the Buddha. It is chanted and often occurs within a sutra.

29 The skillful work hard, the knowledgeable lament and sigh; but those who are unable have nothing for which to seek; they simply eat and do as they wish. They drift along like an unmoored boat, empty and at ease.
—*Chuang Tzu*

30 *Bhutatathata*: The eternal, impersonal, unchangeable reality behind all phenomena. It resembles the ocean in contrast to the waves.

31 Or, the true nature of all things; i.e., the Buddha-nature.

32 Tao Yuan-ming (365–427)

33 Source unknown.

34 A Confucian scholar of the Northern Sung Dynasty (1011–77)

35 The mild and cooing doves fly high and live in the sky.
—*Shih Ching*

36 A Zen Buddhist of the T'ang period.

37 Shao Yao-fu (1011–77), a Neo-Confucian philosopher of the Northern Sung Dynasty. Much interested in numerology. Lived in poverty and was held in deep respect by his neighbors, young and old.

38 The Western Tsin Dynasty, 265–316 A.D.

39 A cemetery north of the old Chinese capital of Loyang, well known for the nobility and famous people buried there.

40 In the third century B.C., the state of Yen attacked the state of Ch'i, the former's army being vastly superior in size. A market official by the name of T'ien T'an was eventually selected as general to organize the defense of the Chi-mo garrison. The outlook for the defenders was grim, but one night T'ien T'an rounded up over a thousand head of oxen, covered them with red silk upon which dragons had been painted, tied knives to their horns and reed torches to their tails. Dousing the torches with oil and igniting them,

the Ch'i army drove the oxen into the midst of the terrified Yen forces, who were routed and destroyed.

41 Confucius said, "Fish cannot leave the water, and man cannot leave the Way. That which cannot leave the water may receive sustenance from a manmade pond; that which cannot leave the Way may live sufficiently without anything much to do." Thus, it is said that "The fish forgets about its mutual existence with the lake, and man forgets about his mutual existence with the practice of the Way."

—*Chuang Tzu*

42 Thus, he who knows Heaven's pleasures will have no grudges with nature, no accusations from others, no external afflictions, and no punishment from the supernatural.

—*Chuang Tzu*

43 The True Men of ancient times did not see dreams when they slept and had no anxieties when awake. They did not consider what they ate to be savory, but their breathing was deep. The breathing of True Men comes from their heels, while that of the majority of men comes from their throats. Those who completely submit themselves [to worldly ways] breathe as though vomiting words; those practiced in deep desire have a shallow sense of what Heaven performs.

—*Chuang Tzu*

44 People eat beef and pork, deer eat hay; the centipedes consider snakes to be sweet, and kites and crows relish mice. Each of the four knows which taste is correct.

—*Chuang Tzu*

45 Those who recite the sutras but do not see the significance of being and non-being, are truly like a man who, riding the donkey, still goes in search of it.

—*Ching-te Ch'uan-teng-lu* (*Record Concerning the Transmission of the Lamp, [Composed in] the Cheng-te period.* Earliest historical work of Zen literature, composed of anecdotes and biographies of early Zen masters. Written by Tao-hsuan, c. 1004 A.D.)

46 A bridge that spanned the Pa River, east of the ancient capital of Ch'ang An. When seeing off travelers, friends would go with them as far as this bridge, and there break off willow branches as a farewell gesture.

47 Lake Chien (Mirror Lake) in the Shaohsing area of Chekiang Province.

48 When the lid on a man's coffin is finally fastened down, his affairs are finally understood. You, My Lord, are happily not yet among the elderly.

—Tu Fu

49 Lao Tzu said, "Men of clever wisdom and saintliness—I do my best to avoid being like them. If in the past you had called me a cow, then I'd have thought of myself as a cow. If you had called me a horse, I would have thought of myself as a horse. The reality exists and men give it a name. If you do not accept that,

you'll be open to receiving twice the disaster."

—*Chuang Tzu*

50 The man who has arrived uses his mind like a mirror: he does not go out to greet things, neither does he respond by storing them away. Thus he is able to receive things, but incurs no harm.

—*Chuang Tzu*

51 Every time K'ai Chih ate sugar cane, he would eat it from the top right down to the root. People thought this was a bit strange, but he said, "This way, you gradually get into the significance of the thing."

—*Chin Shu* (History of the Chin Dynasty [265–420 A.D.]. Compiled at the order of Sung-Dynasty emperor T'ai Tsung.)

52 One of China's most dearly beloved poets; thrived during the T'ang period (772–846).

53 It is not necessarily in the stringed instruments or flutes;
It is in the clear sound of the mountains and rivers.

—*Tso Chuan*

54 A reference to the Seven Sages of the Bamboo Grove.

55 A reference to Tao Yuan-ming's prose poem, *Peach Blossom Spring.*

56 A quote from Shao Yao-fu.

57 If you stand before the center of this and not ask about the village of hermit-wizards, where will you look for the city of flowers?

—*Chuan Chieh* (Collection of Han-period poetry)

58 With three cups, you pass along the Great Way;
With a good bit more, you unite with the Of-Itself-So.
You can only get this when you're drunk.
Don't relate it to those who are sober.

—Li Po

59 A poet of the Sung Dynasty (1053–1110).

60 Both references to Tao Yuan-ming's *Peach Blossom Spring.*

61 The gentleman uses things; the small-minded man is used by things.

—*Hsun Tzu*

62 The man who does not look at himself but looks at others, will not grasp what he himself has, but only what others have. He enjoys what is appropriate to others, but not what is appropriate to himself.

—*Chuang Tzu*

63 Before your father and mother were born,
What was your original face?

—Zen saying

Listen, I have no idea whose child it is.
They were formed before the gods.

—*Tao Te Ching*

Note: This section of the *Tao Te Ching* is about the Tao. But you could as well substitute "you" or "I" for "it" in the first line.

Look, the Way has both reality and manifestations, but does not act and has no form. You can receive it, but cannot transmit it; you can obtain it, but cannot see it. It has its own source and its own root.

Before Heaven and Earth existed, it had been firm and right there since ancient of days. It gave divinity to both the gods and the Universal Emperor; it gave birth to Heaven and Earth. It existed before the Great Ultimate, but you could not say it is high; it is below the Six Directions, but you could not call it low. It was before Heaven and Earth, but you could not say it's been around for a long time. Its time is longer than ancient times, but you could not call it old.

—*Chuang Tzu*

64 The Chinese believed that all things—rocks no less than bamboo—are composed of *ch'i*, that matter-energy that pervades and makes up the universe. They still believe that *ch'i* transforms into the Ten Thousand Things, which themselves are in constant transformation. Thus, rocks "grow" and "decline" like everything else. In *The Mustard Seed Garden Manual of Painting*, written less than a hundred years after Hung Ying-ming, it says that "rocks have *ch'i*. Rocks without *ch'i* are dead rocks. How could a cultivated person paint a lifeless rock?"

65 The single cloud, the wild crane—
How would they live in the midst of men?

—Liu Chang-liu (T'ang-Dynasty poet. Dates uncertain.)

66 My own drifting along: what is it like?
The lone gull on the beach between Heaven and Earth.

—Tu Fu

67 "The other side." I.e., Nirvana.

68 Raindrops on Mount T'ai wear through stone, and a simple well-rope will cut through the well crib. It's not that water will penetrate stone, or that a rope will saw through a tree, but they must naturally affect a gradual transformation.

—*Han Shu* (*History of the Former Han Dynasty*. Written by Pan Ku, 32–92 A.D.)

69 I made myself a hut within human borders,
But there is no noise of wagon or horse.
You ask me how this can be so.
When the mind is far away, the land follows of itself.
Picking chrysanthemums under the eastern hedge,
I leisurely look at the southern mountains.
The spirit of the mountains is excellent day and night;
Birds return, flying two by two.
Within all this there is a deep meaning,
But when I want to explain, I have already forgotten the words.

—Tao Yuan-ming

70 It is recorded in the *Book of the Later Han* that when reed ashes placed in a bamboo pipe flew out of the pipe, the winter solstice had arrived.

71 The withering forces of fall.

72 Climbing the eastern embankment,
I leisurely sing some lines;
Facing the clear currents,
I compose new poems.

—Tao Yuan-ming

73 Identified by Imai Saburo, this

group includes wild parsley, wild asparagus, bracken, and a kind of rhubarb.

74 The gentleman's learning: it comes through his ears and adheres to his mind. It enriches his four limbs and appears in his movements. Even that which is said in whispers, and that which moves in small eddies —with the single example, he can make the rule. The small-minded man's learning: it enters through his ears and goes out through his mouth. Even though there are only four inches between mouth and ears, it is somehow enough to beautify a six-foot body.
—Hsun Tzu

75 Be careful when dealing with the brokers of village and town.
—Shih Chi

76 Ts'ao Sung (d. 867?), a poet of the T'ang Dynasty.

77 Source unknown.

78 I.e., the temples.

79 Taoist term for the Original Mind.

80 He who has exhausted the Way and dies has lived to his natural destiny. He who dies in chains has not lived to his natural destiny.
—Mencius

81 The legendary emperor Fu Hsi; an example of the simplicity of extreme antiquity.

82 Chi K'ang and Yuan Chih: they were two of the Seven Sages of the Bamboo Grove.

83 The gentleman bases himself in his position and acts accordingly; he does not look beyond this. If he is based in wealth and status, he acts in accordance with wealth and status; if he is based in poverty and low station, he acts in accordance with poverty and low station; if he is based among the barbarians, he acts in accordance with being among the barbarians; if he is based in pain and difficulty, he acts in accordance with pain and difficulty. The gentleman is not in any situation where he cannot be himself.
—Doctrine of the Mean

AFTERWORD

1 Josetsu (如拙). 1386–1428. Possibly an immigrant to Japan from China, and considered the father of Zen *suiboku* (monochrome India ink) painting.

BIBLIOGRAPHY

Primary Sources

Kamiko Tadashi, Yoshida Yutaka, eds. *Saikontan*. Tokyo: Tokuma Shoten, 1982.

Imai Saburo, ed. *Saikontan*. Tokyo: Meitoku Shuppansha, 1969.

———*Saikontan*. Tokyp: Iwanami Shoten, 1982.

Shaku Soen, ed. *Saikontan Kowa*. Tokyo: Kyobunsha, 1939.

Secondary Sources

Aoki Masaru, ed. *Rihaku*. Kanshi Taikei, vol. 8. Tokyo: Shueisha, 1965.

Fujii Sen'ei, ed. *Kanpishi*, 2 vols. Tokyo: Meiji Shoin, 1974.

Fukunaga Mitsuji, Kozen Hiroshi, eds. *Roshi/Soshi*. Tokyo: Chikuma Shobo, 2004.

Funatsu Tomihiko, ed. *Sahreiun*. Tokyo: Shueisha, 1974.

Hirata Takashi, ed. *Mumonkan*. Tokyo: Chikuma Shobo, 1969.

Hiro Sachiya, ed. *Saikontan no yomikata*. Tokyo: Nihon Keizai Shinbunsha, 1986.

Ikkai Tomoyoshi, ed. *Toenmei*. Tokyo: Iwanami Shoten, 1958.

Iriya Yoshitaka, ed. *Hanshan*. Tokyo: Iwanami Shoten, 1958.

Kanaya Osamu, ed. *Rongo*. Tokyo: Iwanami Shoten, 1973.

———*Soshi*, 4 vols. Iwanami Shoten, 1983.

Kobayashi Katsuhito, ed. *Moshi*, 2 vols. Tokyo: Iwanami Shoten, 1976.

Kobayashi Nobuaki, ed. *Resshi*. Tokyo: Meiji Shoin, 1967.

Nagao Gajin, ed. *Daijo Butten*, vol. 7. Tokyo: Chuokoronsha, 1975.

Ogawa Tamaki, Yamamoto Kazuyoshi, eds. *Sotoba Shisen*. Tokyo: Iwanami Shoten, 1976.

Okudaira Takashi, Omura Masuo, eds. *Roshi, Resshi*. Tokyo: Iwanami Shoten, 1976.

Shimada Kenji, ed. *Daigaku/chuyo*. Tokyo: Asahi Shinbunsha, 1967.

Suzuki Torao, ed. *To Shi*, vols. 1 & 5. Tokyo: Iwanami Shoten, 1975.

Takada Shinji, ed. *Shi Kyo*. Kanshi Taikei, vols. 1 & 2. Tokyo: Shueisha, 1968.

Takada Shinji, Goto Motomi, eds. *Eki Kyo*, 2 vols. Tokyo: Iwanami Shoten, 1976.

Takeuchi Teruo, ed. *Kanpishi*, vol. 1.

Tokyo: Meiji Shoin, 1963.

Tsuru Haruo, ed. *Toenmei*. Tokyo: Chikuma Shoten, 1974.

Secondary Sources in English

Cahill, James. *Chinese Painting*. New York: Rizzoli International Publications, 1977.

de Bary, William Theodore, and the Conference on Ming Thought. *Self and Society in Ming Thought*. New York: Columbia University Press, 1970.

de Bary, William Theodore, ed. *Sources of Chinese Tradition*. New York: Columbia University Press, 1960.

Fairbank, John K., & Edwin O. Reishauer. *East Asia: Tradition and Transformation*. Boston: Houghton Mifflin Co., 1978.

Goodrich, L. Carrington, & Fang Chao-ying, eds. *Dictionary of Ming Biography, 1368–1644*. New York: Columbia University Press, 1976.

Kato Shuichi. *A History of Japanese Literature: The Years of Isolation*. Tokyo: Kodansha International, 1983.

Liu, James J. Y. *Chinese Theories of Literature*. Chicago: University of Chicago Press, 1975.

Liu, James J. Y. *The Art of Chinese Poetry*. Chicago: University of Chicago Press, 1962.

Munro, Donald J. *The Concept of Man in Early China*. Stanford: Stanford University Press, 1969.

Putzar, Edward, ed. *Japanese Literature: A Historical Outline*. Tucson: University of Arizona Press, 1973.

Sansom, G. B. *Japan, A Short Cultural History*. New York: Appleton-Century-Crofts, Inc., 1943.

Watson, Burton. *Early Chinese Literature*. New York: Columbia University, 1962.

Yoshida Kogoro. *Tanrokubon: Rare Books of the Seventeenth Century*. Tokyo: Kodansha International, 1984.

(英文版) 改訂版 菜根譚 The Unencumbered Spirit

2009年9月28日　第1刷発行

著　者　洪自誠
英　訳　ウィリアム・スコット・ウィルソン
発行者　廣田 浩二
発行所　講談社インターナショナル株式会社
〒112-8652 東京都文京区音羽1-17-14
電話　03-3944-6493（編集部）
　　　03-3944-6492（営業部・業務部）
ホームページ　www.kodansha-intl.com

印刷・製本所　大日本印刷株式会社

定価はカバーに表示してあります。

Printed in Japan
ISBN 978-4-7700-3097-9

落丁本・乱丁本は購入書店名を明記のうえ、講談社インターナショナル業務部宛にお送りください。送料小社負担にてお取替えします。なお、この本についてのお問い合わせは、編集部宛にお願いいたします。本書の無断複写（コピー）、転載は著作権法の例外を除き、禁じられています。

